DEDICATION

To every teenager who has ever doubted their worth or questioned their potential—this book is for you.

This book is for teenagers who struggle in English, math, or any subject and feel they are falling behind—this book is for you.

To the teenager who was told they would never amount to anything—this book is for you.

This book is for teenagers who do not speak English as their first language and face the added challenge of expressing themselves in a new world.

May you find the strength to rise above doubts, embrace your true self, and unlock the greatness within you.

To my family and friends, thank you for your unwavering love and support. To the mentors and teachers who believed in me when I struggled to believe in myself, thank you for lifting me up when I needed it most.

And to the brave souls who have confronted setbacks and challenges head-on—may your resilience inspire others to continue pushing forward. You are stronger, braver, and more capable than you realize.

I believe in you. Keep rising. Keep thriving.

CONTENTS

RISE
ABOVE

TEN WAYS TO STRENGTHEN YOUR MINDSET AS A TEENAGER

BOBBY C. COBB JR.

ABOUT THE AUTHOR

Meet Bobby Cobb: Your Ultimate Guide to Overcoming Self-Doubt and Building Confidence

I wrote "Rise Above: Ten Ways to Strengthen Your Mindset as a Teenager" because I know what it's like to face personal and physical setbacks as a teenager and how they can affect your mindset. I want to provide the guidance and tools needed for pessimistic middle and high school students who feel like giving up to rise above their challenges and thrive confidently.

With my experience as a public servant, a U.S. Navy veteran, the CEO and Founder of Cobb Global Outreach (CGO), INC, a TBI survivor, and a mentor to middle and high school students, CGO Inc. provides financial literacy education to students and offer scholarships. Through my organization, I have significantly impacted students' lives and have firsthand knowledge of their struggles. Additionally, with a Bachelor's in Computer Information Systems and a Master's in Public Administration-General Government, I am uniquely qualified to help students improve their self-confidence and self-esteem.

I encourage you to read "Rise Above" and begin your journey towards improved self-confidence and mindset. Let my experiences and guidance inspire you to conquer doubts and achieve your goals.

INTRODUCTION

Hey there! First off, let me say that I am thrilled that you've decided to pick up a copy of "Rise Above: Ten Ways to Strengthen Your Mindset as A Teenager." You've already taken the first step toward improving your mindset, and I commend you for that. Trust me, I know it's not easy to make that choice when feeling down on yourself and full of doubt. But here's the thing: you've got this. And this book is going to help you every step of the way.

Let's start by addressing the elephant in the room. You're not alone. Many people experience feeling like failure and struggling with self-doubt, especially during the rollercoaster ride that is middle and high school. But here's the good news—you can change your mindset and rise above those negative thoughts. And that's precisely what "Rise Above" is all about.

As the founder of Cobb Global Outreach (CGO) Inc., a Navy Veteran, speaker, motivator, and someone who has overcome their own challenges, I've packed this book with practical advice, tips, tricks, and examples to help guide you through your journey. I draw on my own experiences and education, including my M.P.A. in General Government from Columbus State University and my experience as a traumatic brain injury (TBI) survivor, to provide you with the tools you need to build confidence and self-esteem while avoiding the pitfalls of negative thinking.

I want to assure you that this book is not about making you feel guilty about your negative thoughts or telling you to "think positive." It's about recognizing, challenging, and reframing negative thoughts in a way that sets you up for future success. It's about giving you the tools to build resilience and confidence to carry you through your school years and life.

So, what are you waiting for? Crack open the cover and dive into "Rise Above." It's time to embrace a mindset that will set you up for a lifetime of success. You've got this! Let's do this together.

CHAPTER ONE

COMPARING YOURSELF TO OTHERS

"The only person you should try to be better than is who you were yesterday." – Matty Mullins

Learning Objectives

After completing this chapter, you will be able to:

▶▶ Identify when you're falling into the comparison trap

▶▶ Understand why comparing yourself to others hinders personal growth

> ⇉ Implement specific strategies to focus on your progress
> ⇉ Develop techniques for celebrating your unique journey
> ⇉ Create a personal action plan for building self-confidence

Introduction

Madison sits in her room scrolling through Instagram, her heart sinking with each swipe. Everyone seems to have it all figured out: Sarah just won another academic award, James made the varsity team, and Emma's art was featured in a local gallery. With each post, Madison feels smaller, less accomplished, and increasingly uncertain about her own worth. Does this sound familiar?

Comparing ourselves to others is a natural human tendency, but it can become overwhelming and destructive in today's hyper-connected world. This chapter will help you understand why these comparisons are harmful and provide practical strategies to break free from this habit.

The Dangers of Comparison

First and foremost, comparing yourself to others can lead to a skewed perception of reality. In our digital age, we're constantly bombarded with carefully curated highlights of others' lives. We often forget that we're comparing our behind-the-scenes footage to everyone else's highlight reel. What you see on the surface is usually not the whole picture. People showcase their successes and hide their struggles, making it seem like everyone else is doing better than you. This can lead to feelings of inadequacy and self-doubt, which are significant barriers to personal growth.

Additionally, everyone is on a unique journey with their strengths and weaknesses. Comparing yourself to others can cause you to fail to recognize your unique qualities and the progress you have made. This can create a sense of hopelessness and prevent you from acknowledging and celebrating your achievements.

The Negative Mindset Trap

Constantly comparing yourself to others can foster a negative mindset. When you focus on what others have that you don't, it becomes challenging to see your own potential and the opportunities available to you. This mindset can lead to a cycle of envy and jealousy, further damaging your relationships and hindering your ability to build a supportive network.

Times of Vulnerability

Middle and high school are times of significant change and development. Whether transitioning to a new school, facing academic challenges, or navigating social dynamics, these periods can make you feel insecure and more susceptible to comparison. Recognizing these vulnerable moments is the first step in understanding why and when you might fall into the comparison trap.

Shifting Your Focus: The Path to Growth

The key to building confidence and self-esteem is focusing on your own progress and growth instead of comparing yourself to others. By setting realistic goals for yourself and celebrating your achievements, you can develop a positive mindset and recognize your unique journey.

Setting Achievable Goals

Start by setting small, attainable goals. These could be academic, social, or personal. You can make consistent progress and build momentum by breaking down larger goals into smaller steps. Celebrate each milestone, no matter how small, to reinforce a sense of accomplishment and boost your confidence.

Surrounding Yourself with Positivity

The company you keep plays a significant role in shaping your mindset. Surround yourself with positive influences who support and encourage you. Seek out mentors and role models who can provide guidance and inspiration. Avoid those who consistently make you feel inferior or unworthy.

Embracing Your Unique Journey

Remember that your journey is uniquely yours. Everyone progresses at their own pace, and honoring your path is important. Embrace your strengths and work on your weaknesses without measuring up to others. Your value is not determined by how you compare to others but by your growth and the person you are becoming.

Practical Steps to Implement This Mindset

1. Reflect on Your Achievements: Reflect on your achievements so far. Write down your achievements and acknowledge the hard work and dedication it took to achieve them.

2. Set Personal Goals: Establish clear, realistic goals for yourself. Focus on areas for improvement and create a plan to achieve them. Track your progress and adjust as needed.

3. Practice Gratitude: Keep a gratitude journal where you regularly write down things you are thankful for. This practice can shift your focus from what you lack to what you have, fostering a more positive outlook.

4. Seek Feedback: Constructive feedback from teachers, coaches, and mentors can provide valuable insights into your progress and areas for improvement. Use this feedback to grow and develop further.

5. Limit Social Media Exposure: social media can be a breeding ground for comparison. Limit exposure to these platforms and remind yourself that what you see online is often a curated highlight reel, not the whole story.

Overcoming Past Mistakes

If you find yourself stuck in the comparison trap, it's essential to acknowledge that everyone makes mistakes, and it's never too late to change your mindset. Here are steps you can take to overcome this habit:

1. Recognize the Pattern: Acknowledge when and why you compare yourself to others. Understanding the triggers can help you address them more effectively.

2. Reframe Negative Thoughts: When you catch yourself comparing, reframe the thought by focusing on your progress and what you can do to improve.

3. Seek Professional Help: If comparison and self-doubt significantly impact your mental health, consider talking to a counselor or therapist who can provide strategies to cope and build self-esteem.

#1 Piece of Advice

Comparing yourself to others is a common but detrimental habit that can hinder your personal growth and confidence. By shifting your focus to your progress and development, setting realistic goals, and positively surrounding yourself, you can overcome self-doubt and build a stronger, more resilient mindset. Remember, your journey is unique, and your value is inherent. Embrace your path, celebrate your achievements, and strive for personal excellence.

Reflection Questions:

1. What triggers your comparison thoughts?
2. How can you celebrate your unique qualities?
3. What would change if you stopped comparing yourself to others?
4. How can you support others while staying focused on your own growth?
5. What personal standards would make you proud to achieve?

Chapter Summary

▶ Comparing yourself to others can lead to feelings of inadequacy and a negative mindset.

▶ Focus on your own progress and growth to build confidence and self-esteem.

▶ Set realistic goals, reflect on your achievements, and practice gratitude.

▶ Surround yourself with positive influences and seek constructive feedback.

▶ Overcome past mistakes by recognizing patterns, reframing negative thoughts, and seeking professional help.

By embracing these principles, you can confidently navigate the challenges of middle and high school and emerge stronger, ready to achieve your full potential. However, dwelling on past failures can hinder your potential for growth and advancement. Let's explore the impact of dwelling on past failures and how to overcome this common mistake in pursuing self-improvement. Keep reading to discover how to overcome this obstacle and continue the path to success.

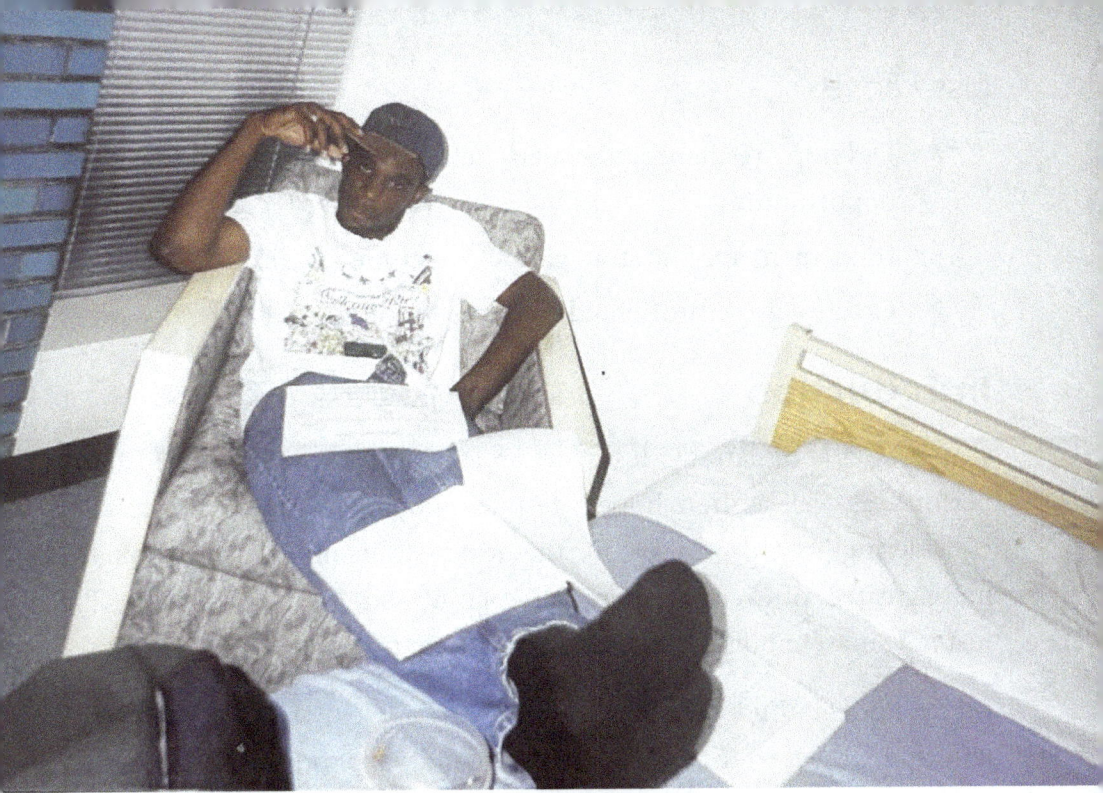

CHAPTER TWO

DWELLING ON PAST FAILURES

"Success is not final, failure is not fatal: it is the courage to continue that counts." - Winston Churchill

Learning Objectives

After completing this chapter, you will be able to:

▶▶ Understand the difference between learning from failure and dwelling on it

▶▶ -dentify patterns of negative self-talk related to past mistakes

> ▷ Develop resilience through reframing failures as learning opportunities
> ▷ Implement specific strategies to overcome setbacks
> ▷ Create a growth-oriented response to future challenges

Introduction

James stares at his latest C-test score and feels his stomach sink. He didn't perform as well as he'd hoped despite studying for hours. Instead of considering how to improve for the next test, his mind races through a highlight reel of every academic disappointment he's experienced. "I'm just not smart enough," he thinks. "Why even try?"

Many students find themselves trapped in a cycle of dwelling on past failures. However, how we interpret and respond to setbacks can significantly impact our future success. This chapter will help you transform your relationship with failure and develop resilience.

Why Dwelling on Past Failures is a Mistake

Dwelling on past failures keeps students stuck in a negative mindset. When they constantly focus on their failures, they cannot see their potential and the opportunities for growth and success right before them. This can lead to a downward spiral of self-doubt and low self-esteem, making breaking free from the cycle of failure even harder.

Lack of Resilience and Coping Skills

Students dwell on past failures because they may lack the resilience and coping skills to bounce back. Instead of seeing failure as a learning opportunity, they see it as a reflection of their abilities and worth. This can lead to feelings of inadequacy and helplessness, further perpetuating a negative mindset.

Fixed Mindset

Another reason students struggle with dwelling on past failures is that they may have a fixed mindset. This means they believe their abilities and talents are set in stone and cannot change or improve. When they experience failure, they see it as evidence of their limitations rather than an opportunity to grow and learn.

Understanding a Fixed Mindset

A fixed mindset is the belief that your abilities, intelligence, and talents are static traits that cannot be developed or improved over time. This perspective suggests that you are born with a certain amount of intelligence or talent, and no amount of effort can change that. People with a fixed mindset tend to avoid challenges, give up quickly, and see effort as fruitless because they believe their capabilities are predetermined.

The Impact of a Fixed Mindset on Students

A fixed mindset can be particularly damaging for middle and high school students. When they encounter failure or setbacks, they may interpret these experiences as a reflection of their inherent limitations. Instead of viewing failure as a chance to learn and grow, they see it as proof that they lack the necessary skills or intelligence to succeed.

This belief can lead to:

Avoidance of Challenges: Students with a fixed mindset may avoid new and difficult tasks because they fear failure and do not want to expose their perceived weaknesses. This avoidance prevents them from developing new skills and gaining valuable experiences.

Negative Self-Perception: Experiencing failure can reinforce negative beliefs about oneself. Students may view themselves as incapable or "not smart enough," which can erode their self-esteem and confidence over time.

Lack of Effort: If students believe that effort will not improve their abilities, they are less likely to put in the hard work necessary to improve. This can lead to poor academic performance and missed growth opportunities.

Increased Anxiety and Stress: The fear of failure and the pressure to prove themselves can create significant anxiety and stress. Students may feel they must constantly prove their worth, leading to burnout and emotional exhaustion.

Shifting to a Growth Mindset

To counter the negative effects of a fixed mindset, it is essential to cultivate a growth mindset. A growth mindset is the belief that abilities and intelligence can be developed through dedication, hard work, and perseverance.

Embracing a growth mindset involves:

Viewing Challenges as Opportunities: Instead of avoiding strenuous tasks, students with a growth mindset see challenges as chances to learn and grow. They understand that overcoming obstacles can lead to personal development and improved skills.

Embracing Effort: Effort is seen as a path to mastery. Students recognize that hard work and persistence are key factors in achieving success and are willing to invest the time and energy to improve.

Learning from Criticism: Constructive feedback is welcomed as a valuable tool for growth. Students with a growth mindset use criticism to identify areas for improvement and make the necessary adjustments to enhance their performance.

Finding Inspiration in Others: Rather than feeling threatened by others' success, students with a growth mindset are inspired by their peers' achievements. They understand that learning from others can provide valuable insights and motivate them to strive for their own success.

Practical Steps to Develop a Growth Mindset

1. Acknowledge and Challenge Fixed Mindset Thoughts: When facing challenges, pay attention to negative thoughts. Replace statements like "I'm not good at this" with "I can improve with practice."

2. Set Learning Goals Instead of Performance Goals: Focus on what you can learn and how you can grow rather than solely on the outcome. This shift in perspective encourages continuous improvement and reduces the fear of failure.

3. Celebrate Effort and Progress: Recognize and celebrate the effort you put into tasks, regardless of the final result. This reinforces the idea that hard work and perseverance are valuable and practical.

4. Learn from Mistakes: View mistakes as opportunities to learn. Reflect on what went wrong, what you can do differently next time, and how to apply these lessons to future challenges.

5. Seek Feedback: Ask teachers, peers, and mentors for feedback. Use this feedback to identify areas for improvement and guide your efforts toward growth.

6. Surround Yourself with Growth-Oriented Individuals: Engage with people with a growth mindset who support your efforts to learn and improve. Positive influences can reinforce your commitment to personal development.

By shifting from a fixed mindset to a growth mindset, students can transform their approach to challenges and setbacks. This change in perspective fosters resilience, encourages continuous learning, and ultimately leads to greater confidence and success in academic and personal endeavors.

Real-life Example of a Fixed Mindset

Meet Emily: A Student Struggling with a Fixed Mindset

Emily is a high school sophomore who has always considered herself a "math person." In middle school, she excelled in math, earning top grades with minimal effort. However, high school math has proven to be much more challenging for her.

Encountering a Challenge

In her sophomore year, Emily is enrolled in an advanced algebra class. The concepts are more complex, and the pace is faster than she's used to. For the first time, Emily struggles to keep up with the material. She failed her first major test, scoring significantly lower than she expected. This experience is a blow to her self-esteem.

The Fixed Mindset Response

Because Emily has a fixed mindset, she interprets this failure as a sign that she isn't as good at math as she thought. Her internal dialogue goes something like this:

- ▶ "I'm just not smart enough to handle this math level."
- ▶ "I've never had to work this hard before; maybe I'm just not cut out for it."
- ▶ "If I were good at math, I wouldn't struggle like this."

These thoughts lead Emily to feel anxious and discouraged. Instead of seeking help or trying different study strategies, she avoids math homework and disengages in class discussions. She doesn't ask questions because she fears looking dumb in front of her peers. Her grades continue to decline, reinforcing her belief that she cannot succeed in advanced math.

Consequences of a Fixed Mindset

Emily's fixed mindset has several negative consequences:

Avoidance of Effort: Emily stops putting in the necessary effort because she believes it won't make a difference. Her fear of confirming her perceived inadequacies makes her reluctant to try.

Lack of Improvement: Emily's skills stagnate without effort and the willingness to seek help. She misses out on opportunities to learn and grow.

Decreased Confidence: Her self-confidence plummets as she becomes more convinced that she cannot succeed in math.

Increased Anxiety: The stress and anxiety about her perceived limitations make the learning process even more challenging and unpleasant.

The Shift to a Growth Mindset

To help Emily shift to a growth mindset, her teacher and parents encourage her to see failure as a learning opportunity rather than a reflection of her abilities. Here's how they support her:

1. Reframe Failure: Emily's teacher explains that failure is a natural part of the learning process, and everyone struggles with new and challenging material. They encourage her to view mistakes as opportunities to learn.

2. Celebrate Effort: Emily's parents praise her for the effort she puts into studying and remind her that hard work and persistence are vital to mastering complex subjects. They celebrate minor improvements and progress rather than just high grades.

3. Provide Resources: Emily's teacher offers additional resources, such as tutoring sessions, online tutorials, and study groups. They encourage her to ask questions and participate actively in class.

4. Set Learning Goals: Instead of focusing solely on grades, Emily sets specific learning goals, such as understanding a particular concept or improving her problem-solving skills. This shift helps her focus on the process rather than just the outcome.

5. Model Growth Mindset: Her teacher and parents share their experiences with failure and how they overcame challenges through perseverance and learning. This helps Emily see that struggling is normal and that growth is possible.

Outcome

Over time, Emily begins to adopt a growth mindset. She starts to see that effort leads to improvement and that her abilities can develop with hard work. She becomes more willing to seek help and try new study strategies. Her grades gradually improve, but more importantly, she gains confidence in learning and growing.

By shifting from a fixed mindset to a growth mindset, Emily transforms her approach to challenges and setbacks. She becomes more resilient, willing to take risks, and motivated to achieve her goals. This change improves her math performance and sets her up for long-term success in other areas of her life.

Fear of Failure

The fear of failure is a common and powerful emotion that can significantly impact a student's mindset and behavior. This fear often causes students to dwell on past mistakes and avoid taking risks, stifling their growth and success. Let's explore this concept further.

Why Fear of Failure is Detrimental

1. Avoidance of Risks:

Limited Experiences: Students who fear failure often avoid trying new things or stepping out of their comfort zones. This means they miss valuable experiences that could help them learn and grow.

Stagnation: By not taking risks, students stay within their known capabilities, which limits their development and hinders the discovery of new talents or interests.

2. Negative Reinforcement:

Cycle of Fear: When students avoid risks and still experience failure, this reinforces their fear. They may believe that failure is unavoidable and that their efforts are pointless.

Low Self-Esteem: Repeated avoidance and negative reinforcement can decrease self-esteem and confidence. Students begin to see themselves as incapable, further entrenching their fear of failure.

3. Missed Opportunities:

Academic Growth: Students who fear failure may avoid challenging subjects or advanced classes, missing opportunities for educational growth and achievement.

Extracurricular Activities: They might avoid joining clubs, sports teams, or other extracurricular activities that would allow them to excel and build new skills.

Social Development: Fear of failure can also impact social interactions, as students may avoid making new friends or participating in group activities.

Real-Life Example of Fear of Failure

Meet Sarah: A Student Paralyzed by Fear of Failure

Sarah is a high school junior who has always excelled academically. She is known for her high grades and dedication to her studies. However, Sarah's fear of failure has become a significant barrier to her growth and well-being.

Encountering a Challenge

Sarah is invited to join the school's debate team, a prestigious group that competes at the state level. Although she is interested and knows it could be a great opportunity, Sarah is terrified of the possibility of failure. She worries about not performing well and embarrassing herself in front of her peers.

The Fearful Response

Sarah's fear leads her to decline the invitation despite her interest. Her internal dialogue includes thoughts like:

- "What if I'm not good enough and I fail?"
- "Everyone will think I'm a fraud if I make a mistake."
- "I can't handle the pressure of competing."

By avoiding this opportunity, Sarah misses the chance to develop her public speaking skills, learn to construct arguments and build confidence in her abilities. Her fear of failure keeps her stuck in her comfort zone, reinforcing the belief that she should avoid situations where she might fail.

Consequences of Fear of Failure

1. Missed Opportunities for Growth:

Academic Stagnation: Sarah avoids taking advanced courses that she might find challenging, sticking to subjects she is comfortable with. This limits her educational development and learning potential.

Social Isolation: She declines invitations to social events or clubs where she might meet new friends, leading to feelings of loneliness and isolation.

2. Increased Anxiety and Stress:

Perfectionism: Sarah's fear of failure contributes to a perfectionist attitude, where she feels immense pressure to perform flawlessly in everything she does. This leads to chronic stress and anxiety.

Procrastination: She often procrastinates on assignments and projects because she fears they will not be perfect. This only increases her stress levels and impacts her performance.

3. Reinforcement of Negative Beliefs:

Low Self-Esteem: Each time Sarah avoids a new challenge, it reinforces her belief that she is incapable. Her self-esteem continues to decline as she perceives herself as a failure.

Lack of Resilience: By not facing her fears, Sarah does not develop the resilience to cope with setbacks and failures. She remains vulnerable to negative experiences and ill-equipped to handle future challenges.

Addressing the Problem with Procrastination

Procrastination is a common issue among middle and high school students. It involves delaying or postponing tasks, often until the last minute, which can lead to increased stress, poor academic performance, and a negative impact on overall well-being. Let's examine the root causes and find solutions to combat procrastination.

Understanding Procrastination

1. Fear of Failure:

Paralyzing Fear: Students may procrastinate because they fear failing at a task. This fear can be so overwhelming that it prevents them from starting the task altogether.

Avoidance Behavior: By delaying the task, they temporarily avoid the anxiety associated with the fear of failure. However, this only increases the pressure as the deadline approaches.

2. Lack of Motivation:

No Immediate Reward: Tasks that do not offer immediate rewards can be hard to start. Students may struggle to see the value in completing a task that does not provide instant gratification.

Interest Levels: Tasks perceived as boring or uninteresting are often put off in favor of more enjoyable activities.

3. Poor Time Management:

Underestimating Time: Students often underestimate the time required to complete a task, leading to last-minute rushes and subpar performance.

Disorganization: Lack of a structured plan or schedule can result in tasks being forgotten or not appropriately prioritized.

4. Perfectionism:

Fear of Imperfection: Students with perfectionist tendencies may procrastinate because they fear their work will not meet their high standards. They delay starting tasks, hoping to find the "perfect" time or conditions.

Overwhelm: The desire for perfect outcomes can be overwhelming, leading to avoidance of tasks altogether.

Consequences of Procrastination

1. Increased Stress and Anxiety:

Last-Minute Rush: Procrastinating until the last minute creates a frantic rush to complete tasks, which can lead to heightened stress and anxiety.

Sleep Deprivation: Pulling all-nighters to finish work can result in sleep deprivation, which can negatively impact health and cognitive function.

2. Poor Academic Performance:

Subpar Work: Rushed work often lacks quality, leading to lower grades and academic performance.

Missed Deadlines: Chronic procrastination can result in missed deadlines, severely impacting academic records.

3. Negative Impact on Self-Esteem:

Feelings of Failure: Continual procrastination can lead to feelings of guilt, failure, and decreased self-worth.

Eroded Confidence: Repeatedly failing to meet expectations can erode students' confidence in their abilities.

Addressing Procrastination: Effective Strategies

1. Break Tasks into Smaller Steps:

Manageable Chunks: Divide larger tasks into smaller, more manageable steps. This makes the task seem less daunting and more accessible to start.

Set Milestones: Create milestones and celebrate small achievements to maintain motivation.

2. Prioritize and Schedule:

Create a Plan: Develop a clear plan or schedule outlining what needs to be done and when. Use tools like planners, calendars, or digital apps to keep track of tasks.

Set Priorities: Determine which tasks are most important and tackle them first.

3. Eliminate Distractions:

Dedicated Workspace: Create a dedicated workspace free from noise, social media, and other interruptions.

Set Boundaries: Establish boundaries for study time and inform friends and family when you will not be disturbed.

4. Use Positive Reinforcement:

Reward System: Implement a reward system for completing tasks. To keep motivation high, rewards can be small, such as a treat or a break.

Positive Self-Talk: Encourage yourself with positive affirmations and remind yourself of past successes.

5. Seek Support:

Accountability Partner: Find a friend, family member, or mentor who can monitor your progress.

Professional Help: If procrastination severely impacts your life, consider seeking help from a counselor or therapist.

Real-Life Example of Overcoming Procrastination

Meet Sarah: A Student Struggling with Procrastination

Sarah is a high school sophomore who consistently struggles with procrastination. She often puts off assignments until the night before they are due, which leads to rushed work and high-stress levels.

Encountering the Problem

Sarah's procrastination begins to affect her grades and mental well-being. She realizes that she needs to make a change but feels overwhelmed by the magnitude of her tasks.

Implementing Solutions

1. Breaking Tasks into Smaller Steps:

Sarah starts breaking down her assignments into smaller tasks. She breaks it into steps for a research paper, such as selecting a topic, researching, outlining, drafting, and revising.

She sets daily goals to complete each step, making the task less intimidating.

2. Prioritizing and Scheduling:

Sarah creates a study schedule that outlines her daily tasks. She prioritizes her most important assignments and tackles them first.

She uses a planner to keep track of deadlines and sets reminders to stay on track.

3. Eliminating Distractions:

Sarah sets up a quiet study space in her room, free from distractions like her phone and social media.

She establishes a study routine, informing her family when she needs uninterrupted time to focus on her work.

4. Using Positive Reinforcement:

Sarah rewards herself with short breaks and treats after completing each task. This helps her stay motivated and focused.

She practices positive self-talk, reminding herself of her progress and past successes.

5. Seeking Support:

Sarah asks a friend to be her accountability partner. They check in with each other regularly to ensure they are staying on track with their assignments.

She also seeks guidance from a school counselor to develop better time management strategies and coping mechanisms.

Outcome

By implementing these strategies, Sarah significantly improves her ability to manage tasks and reduce procrastination. Her stress levels decrease, and her academic performance improves. She feels more in control of her time and is better equipped to handle future challenges.

Conclusion

Procrastination is common among middle and high school students, but it can be effectively managed with the right strategies and mindset. By breaking tasks into smaller steps, prioritizing and scheduling, eliminating distractions, using positive reinforcement, and seeking support, students can overcome procrastination and achieve their goals. It is important to recognize that overcoming procrastination requires patience and persistence. With determination and the right tools, students can develop better time management skills, reduce stress, and improve their overall well-being.

Overcoming the Fear of Failure

1. Reframe Failure:

Learning Opportunity: Encourage students to view failure as a learning opportunity rather than a reflection of their abilities. Emphasize that everyone fails and is a natural part of the learning process.

Growth Mindset: Promote a growth mindset where students understand that abilities can be developed through dedication and hard work.

2. Set Realistic Goals:

Incremental Steps: Help students set small, achievable goals that allow them to experience success and build confidence. Celebrate these successes, no matter how minor they may seem.

Gradual Challenges: Gradually introduce more challenging tasks to help students build resilience and adapt to handling more complex situations.

3. Encourage Risk-Taking:

Safe Environment: Create a supportive environment where students feel safe taking risks and making mistakes. Please encourage them to try new things and leave their comfort zones.

Positive Reinforcement: Provide positive reinforcement and constructive feedback to help students learn from their experiences and feel supported.

4. Provide Support:

Mentorship: Connect students with mentors who can offer guidance and encouragement and share their experiences with failure and success.

Counseling: If fear of failure is significantly impacting a student's well-being, consider recommending counseling or therapy to address underlying anxiety and build coping strategies.

Outcome

By addressing the fear of failure and encouraging a more positive and growth-oriented mindset, students like Sarah can begin to see challenges as opportunities rather than threats. They become more willing to take risks, learn from their mistakes, and ultimately build the resilience and confidence to succeed academically and personally.

Consequences of Dwelling on Past Failures

The consequences of dwelling on past failures are much worse than you might think. When students believe they are failures and succumb to pessimism, it can have terrible, life-ruining effects. This mindset can lead to a lack of motivation, poor academic performance, and a negative impact on mental and emotional well-being.

Limited Potential

Believing you are a failure limits your potential for growth and success. This mindset can lead to a self-fulfilling prophecy, where you fail because you don't believe in yourself and your abilities. This can also lead to missed opportunities and negatively impact relationships with friends, family, and teachers.

The #1 Way to Avoid This Mistake

The best way to avoid dwelling on past failures is to learn from them and use them to propel yourself forward. This approach allows you to turn negative experiences into valuable learning opportunities and grow from them.

Reframe Your Perspective on Failure

To implement this immediately, start by reframing your perspective on failure. Instead of seeing it as a sign of incompetence, view it as a stepping-stone towards improvement. Take the time to reflect on what went wrong and why, and identify the lessons that can be learned from the experience.

Build Confidence Through Achievable Goals

Next, focus on building your confidence by setting small, achievable goals and working towards them. Celebrate your successes, no matter how small they may seem, and use them as motivation to keep moving forward. Surround yourself with positive influences and seek out mentors or role models who can offer guidance and support.

Practical Steps to Implement This Mindset

1. Reflect on Your Mistakes: Understand what went wrong and why. Identify the lessons you can learn from the experience and how you can apply them in the future.

2. Set Achievable Goals: Break down your long-term goals into smaller, manageable steps. Celebrate each small victory and use it to motivate you to keep moving forward.

3. Seek Positive Influences: Surround yourself with supportive friends, family, and mentors who can encourage and guide you. Avoid negative influences that reinforce feelings of failure.

4. Practice Self-Care: Engage in activities that promote mental and emotional well-being, such as exercise, mindfulness, and hobbies. Taking care of yourself can help boost your confidence and resilience.

Overcoming Past Mistakes

If you've already made the mistake of dwelling on past failures, it's important to recognize that it's never too late to turn things around. Here are practical steps to overcome this habit:

1. Seek Mentors and Role Models: Learn from the experiences of those who have overcome similar challenges. Surround yourself with positive influences that can help shift your mindset.

2. Practice Self-Care: Develop healthy habits that promote mental and emotional well-being. This could include exercise, mindfulness practices, and time with supportive friends and family.

3. Set Small Goals: Build confidence by setting small, achievable goals and celebrating your progress. Each small victory can boost your self-esteem and help you develop a positive outlook.

4. Challenge Negative Thoughts: Reframe negative thoughts more positively. Instead of thinking, "I can't do this," try thinking, "I can learn and improve." This shift in mindset can significantly improve one's ability to overcome self-doubt.

Preventing Future Mistakes

To prevent dwelling on past failures in the future, focus on using setbacks as stepping-stones for growth and progress. Acknowledge negative thoughts when they arise, but then challenge and reframe them. Concentrating on your strengths and past successes can build a foundation for future confidence and resilience.

Tools to Get the Job Done Faster, Better, Easier

There are several tools available to help you prevent the mistake of feeling like a failure and instead learn from your mistakes and use them to propel yourself forward:

1. Positive Affirmations: Repeating positive statements about yourself can help rewire your brain to think more positively and build self-confidence.

2. Goal setting: Setting achievable goals and working towards them can give you a sense of accomplishment and boost your self-esteem.

3. Visualization: Visualizing yourself achieving your goals and overcoming obstacles can help build confidence and focus on positive outcomes.

4. Gratitude Journal: Keeping a journal of things you are grateful for can shift your focus from negative thoughts to the positive aspects of your life, helping to build resilience and self-worth.

5. Support System: Surrounding yourself with positive and supportive people who believe in you can encourage and help you overcome self-doubt.

#1 Piece of Advice

Here's my biggest advice on overcoming self-doubt and building confidence in the future: instead of dwelling on your mistakes and allowing them to define you, learn from them and use them to propel yourself forward. As a middle or high school student, it's easy to get caught up in the idea that failure is permanent and signifies a lack of ability or worth. However, this mindset can be incredibly detrimental to your growth and potential.

Learning from your mistakes and using them to propel you forward is important because it allows you to see failure as a learning opportunity rather than a reflection of your worth. By understanding what went wrong and how you can improve in the future, you will build resilience and confidence in your abilities. This approach also helps you develop a growth mindset, which is essential for academic and life success.

I encourage you to take action on what you've learned in this chapter by changing your perspective on failure. Embrace it as an opportunity to learn and grow rather than a sign of inadequacy. As you shift your mindset, you will become more willing to take risks and confidently pursue your goals, knowing that each mistake is simply a stepping stone on your path to success.

Reflection Questions:

1. How has dwelling on past failures affected your choices?
2. What would you attempt if you weren't afraid of failing?
3. How can you better support yourself during challenging times?
4. What resources could help you overcome current obstacles?
5. How might your approach to failure impact your future success?

Chapter Summary

▶ Use self-doubt and failure as stepping stones for growth

▶ Acknowledge and challenge negative thoughts

▶ Focus on strengths and past successes

▶ Reframe perspective and learn from mistakes

▶ Setbacks and challenges are part of the journey but don't define you

As we've discussed, it's essential to learn from our mistakes and use them as fuel for growth. However, it's equally vital to avoid setting unrealistic expectations for ourselves, which we'll discuss in the next chapter. To ensure sustainable progress, keep reading to discover how to navigate this common mistake and continue on your path to success.

CHAPTER THREE

SETTING UNREALISTIC EXPECTATIONS

"Success is not an accident. It is the result of your attitude, and your attitude is a choice. Hence, success is a matter of choice and not chance."
- Shiv Khera

Learning Objectives

After completing this chapter, you will be able to:

▶ Identify unrealistic expectations in your academic and personal life

▶ Understand the difference between challenging goals and unrealistic demands

▶ Develop strategies for setting achievable goals

▶ Create balanced approaches to self-improvement

▶ Implement methods for celebrating progress and small victories

Introduction

Rachel sits at her desk late at night, surrounded by textbooks and study materials. Despite maintaining a 4.0 GPA, participating in three varsity sports, and leading multiple school clubs, she feels as though she isn't doing enough. Her recent B+ on a chemistry test, though still an excellent grade, has left her questioning her abilities. "I should be able to do everything perfectly," she thinks. "Why can't I handle it all?"

Setting high expectations can drive us to achieve great things, but when these expectations become unrealistic, they can lead to burnout, anxiety, and diminished self-worth. This chapter will help you strike a balance between ambitious goals and sustainable expectations.

Why Setting Unrealistic Expectations is a Mistake

Setting unrealistic expectations can be detrimental for several reasons. When you set goals that are too high or unattainable, you set yourself up for failure. This cycle can lead to self-doubt and a persistent feeling of inadequacy.

Leads to a Cycle of Failure

When you consistently fail to meet your overly ambitious goals, it reinforces the belief that you are not capable. This can lead to a lack of motivation as you start to believe that no matter how hard you try, you will never succeed. This mindset can be crippling, preventing you from taking on new challenges or trying new things.

Negatively Impacts Mental Health

Constantly feeling like you're not meeting expectations can have severe negative effects on your mental health. It can lead to chronic stress, anxiety, and even depression. The pressure to meet these unrealistic standards can make it hard to enjoy your achievements, no matter how significant they might be.

Reasons Students Set Unrealistic Expectations

Middle and high school students who struggle with pessimism and feelings of failure often set unrealistic expectations for a few key reasons:

Pressure from External Sources

Students often feel immense pressure from parents, teachers, and peers to excel in all areas. This pressure can push them to set goals that are beyond their current capabilities, in an effort to meet these high expectations.

Fear of Failure

For some, setting unrealistic goals is a way to protect themselves from the fear of failure. By setting the bar so high, they can rationalize their failure as inevitable rather than a reflection of their actual abilities.

Perfectionism

Perfectionists believe that anything less than perfect is unacceptable. This mindset leads them to set unattainable goals, ensuring that they are constantly striving for an impossible standard.

When Students Make This Mistake

This mistake often occurs during pivotal moments in a student's academic and social life. For example, students may set unrealistic expectations for their grades, extracurricular involvement, and social relationships at the start of a new school year. Additionally, during adversity, such as failing a test or facing a setback, students may set unrealistic goals to overcompensate for their perceived failure.

The Importance of Setting Achievable Goals

Instead of setting unrealistic expectations, students should focus on setting achievable goals and celebrating small victories. Students can build confidence and momentum toward their ultimate objectives by breaking down larger goals into smaller, manageable tasks.

Building Confidence

Achievable goals provide clear milestones to reach, which helps build your confidence. Each small victory reinforces the belief that you can progress, which can motivate you to continue working toward larger goals.

Maintaining Motivation

When you set realistic goals, you are more likely to meet them. This success can motivate you as you see tangible evidence of your progress. It also reduces the likelihood of burnout, as you won't constantly push yourself to meet impossible standards.

Practical Steps to Implement This Mindset

1. Set Small, Realistic Goals: Break down your larger objectives into smaller, manageable steps. Instead of getting straight A's in all subjects, focus on improving your grades in one subject at a time.

2. Celebrate Small Victories: Acknowledge and celebrate your achievements, no matter how small they may seem. This could be as simple as treating yourself to your favorite snack or taking a break to do something you enjoy.

3. Track Your Progress: Keep a journal or checklist to track your progress. Seeing how far you've come can motivate and provide a sense of accomplishment.

4. Seek Support: Surround yourself with positive influences that encourage and celebrate your successes. These could be friends, family, teachers, or mentors who can provide guidance and support.

5. Practice Self-Compassion. Be kind to yourself and recognize that progress takes time. Setbacks are a natural part of the journey, and they do not define your worth or abilities.

Overcoming Past Mistakes

If you've already set unrealistic expectations and feel like a failure, you must recognize that you can turn things around. Here are steps to overcome this habit:

1. Reflect on Your Goals: Take a step back and assess whether your goals are realistic. Adjust them if necessary to make them more attainable.

2. Focus on Incremental Progress: Shift your focus from the end goal to the steps you need to take to get there. Celebrate each small victory along the way.

3. Build a Support System: Seek mentors and role models who can offer guidance and encouragement. Surround yourself with people who believe in your potential.

4. Practice Self-Care. Engage in activities that promote mental and emotional well-being. This can help reduce stress and improve your overall outlook.

Preventing Future Mistakes

It's crucial to maintain a balanced perspective to prevent unrealistic expectations in the future. Focus on what you can do in the present rather than dwelling on past failures or worrying about future outcomes. Setting small, attainable goals and celebrating each milestone can build a foundation for long-term success and well-being.

Tools to Help You Succeed

Several tools can help you set achievable goals and celebrate small victories:

1. Positive Affirmations: Start your day with affirmations reinforcing your capabilities and worth.

2. Gratitude Journaling: Keep a gratitude journal to shift your focus from negative thoughts to positive aspects of your life.

3. Self-Compassion Exercises: Practice being kind to yourself and forgiving your mistakes.

4. Visualization Techniques: Picture yourself achieving your goals and the steps you must take.

5. Growth Mindset Resources: Explore books, podcasts, and videos that promote a growth mindset and provide guidance on overcoming self-doubt.

#1 Piece of Advice

My most significant advice for overcoming self-doubt and building confidence is to set achievable goals and celebrate small victories. It's easy to get overwhelmed by the pressures and expectations of school and life, but breaking down your goals into manageable steps can make a huge difference. Celebrating your progress, no matter how small, reinforces your belief in your abilities and keeps you motivated.

Take action by setting realistic goals for yourself and acknowledging your achievements. Surround yourself with supportive people, practice self-compassion, and use positive affirmations and gratitude journaling to stay focused on your progress. Remember, success is a journey made up of small steps. Celebrating each one will build the confidence and resilience needed to achieve your dreams.

Reflection Questions:

1. Which of your current expectations might be unrealistic?
2. How has perfectionism affected your well-being?
3. What would a more balanced approach to achievement look like?
4. Who can support you in maintaining realistic expectations?
5. What small victory can you celebrate today?

Chapter Summary

▷ - Set achievable goals and celebrate small victories.

▷ - Focus on the present moment, not past failures.

▷ - Build confidence by setting small, attainable goals.

▷ - Celebrate each milestone, no matter how small.

▷ - Success is about progress; keep a positive mindset and believe in your ability to succeed.

As we've navigated the importance of setting achievable goals and celebrating small victories, we uncovered the power of self-care in maintaining a healthy and balanced approach to success. In the next chapter, we will delve into the crucial mistake of neglecting self-care and its impact on our overall well-being, offering valuable strategies for prioritizing our own needs. Keep reading to discover how prioritizing self-care can lead to greater success and fulfillment.

CHAPTER FOUR
LACK OF SELF-CARE

"Self-care is not selfish. You cannot serve from an empty vessel." - Eleanor Brown

Learning Objectives

After completing this chapter, you will be able to:

- ▶▶ Recognize the essential role of self-care in maintaining mental and physical well-being
- ▶▶ Identify signs of burnout and stress
- ▶▶ Develop a personalized self-care routine

> ⯈ Implement strategies for maintaining balance in your daily life
> ⯈ Create boundaries that protect your well-being

Introduction

Michael excels in his advanced placement courses and is the debate team captain. From the outside, he appears to have everything under control. However, he regularly stays up until 2 AM studying, skips meals to complete assignments, and hasn't spent time with friends in weeks. Despite his achievements, Michael feels constantly exhausted and increasingly anxious. His story reflects a common challenge among high-achieving students: neglecting self-care to pursue success.

Self-care is the foundation of sustainable achievement and personal well-being. This chapter will help you understand why taking care of yourself is not only important but essential for long-term success and happiness.

Why Lack of Self-Care is a Mistake

Neglecting self-care is a significant mistake because these activities are essential for maintaining physical and mental well-being. When you ignore your basic needs, negative thoughts and feelings of failure can easily take over. Additionally, neglecting self-care can lead to a lack of energy and motivation, making it even harder to break out of the cycle of self-doubt. Finally, failing to prioritize self-care can lead to long-term negative effects on both physical and mental health.

Physical Health Decline

When you don't take care of your body through regular exercise and healthy eating, your physical health can suffer. Lack of exercise can lead to decreased energy and physical fitness, while poor nutrition can affect overall health and cognitive functions. Both of these can contribute to feelings of fatigue and reduced ability to cope with stress.

Mental Health Deterioration

Neglecting self-care also negatively impacts your mental health. Without adequate sleep, your brain doesn't get the rest it needs to function correctly, leading to difficulty concentrating, mood swings, and increased stress. Furthermore, without the endorphins that come from regular exercise, your mood can become more hostile, and feelings of anxiety and depression can increase.

Reasons Students Neglect Self-Care

There are several reasons why middle and high school students who are pessimistic and feel like failures make the mistake of neglecting self-care.

Academic and Social Pressures

The pressure to succeed academically and socially can be all-consuming, leaving little time or energy for self-care activities. Many students feel they must sacrifice their well-being to meet these high demands.

Feelings of Unworthiness

Many students struggling with self-doubt feel they don't deserve to prioritize their own well-being. This mindset leads to a cycle of neglect, where they continuously put their needs last, reinforcing their feelings of inadequacy.

Negative Thought Patterns

The negative thought patterns accompanying feelings of failure can make it difficult to see the value of self-care. When one is stuck in a loop of self-criticism and doubt, it can be hard to recognize that taking care of oneself is crucial for breaking out of that cycle.

When Students Make This Mistake

Students tend to make this mistake when they feel overwhelmed by school or social pressures or experiencing a particularly challenging time. Instead of prioritizing self-care, they may turn to unhealthy coping mechanisms such as procrastination, isolation, or self-criticism.

The Importance of Prioritizing Self-Care

Students should prioritize self-care instead of neglecting it. This means making time for activities such as exercise, healthy eating, and proper sleep, even when it feels like there's no time to spare. It is essential to recognize the value of self-care and make a conscious effort to break out of negative thought patterns. Seeking support from trusted friends, family members, or mental health professionals can also be incredibly helpful in overcoming self-doubt and building confidence.

Physical and Mental Well-Being

Prioritizing self-care activities helps maintain physical and mental well-being. Regular exercise releases endorphins, which improve mood and reduce stress. Healthy eating provides the nutrients your body and brain need to function optimally, while proper sleep is crucial for cognitive function and emotional regulation.

Breaking the Cycle of Self-Doubt

By caring for your physical and mental health, you build a foundation for breaking the cycle of self-doubt. Self-care activities boost your energy levels, improve your mood, and enhance your ability to cope with stress, making it easier to develop a positive self-image and build confidence.

Practical Steps to Implement This Mindset

1. Incorporate Exercise: Aim to include at least 30 minutes of physical activity in your daily routine. This could be a workout at the gym, a run outside, or even a yoga session at home.

2. Healthy Eating: Eat a balanced diet with plenty of fruits, vegetables, lean proteins, and whole grains. Plan and prepare healthy meals and snacks to ensure you get the necessary nutrients.

3. Proper Sleep: Establish a bedtime routine that allows for 7-9 hours of quality sleep each night. Avoid screens before bed and engage in calming activities like reading or meditation to create a relaxing environment.

4. Seek Support: Surround yourself with positive influences and supportive relationships. Contact friends, family, or mentors who can provide encouragement and guidance.

Overcoming Past Mistakes

If you've already made the mistake of neglecting self-care, it's important to recognize that it's never too late to turn things around. Here are steps to overcome this habit:

1. Start Small: Incorporate one self-care activity into your daily routine. Gradually add more as you become comfortable.

2. Create a Schedule: Plan your day to include time for exercise, healthy eating, and proper sleep. Consistency is key to making these activities a regular part of your life.

3. Set Realistic Goals: Focus on achievable goals to build confidence. For example, aim to exercise three times a week or eat more fruits and vegetables.

4. Practice Self-Compassion: Be kind to yourself and understand that making changes takes time. Celebrate your progress and forgive yourself for any setbacks.

Preventing Future Mistakes

To prevent neglecting self-care in the future, prioritize these activities in your daily routine. Recognize their importance for your overall well-being and success. Making self-care a habit can build the resilience and confidence needed to face challenges and achieve your goals.

Tools to Help You Succeed

Several tools can help you prioritize self-care and build confidence:

1. Positive Affirmations: Start your day with affirmations reinforcing your worth and capabilities.

2. Gratitude Journaling: Keep a gratitude journal to shift your focus from negative thoughts to positive aspects of your life.

3. Self-Compassion Exercises: Practice being kind to yourself and forgiving your mistakes.

4. Visualization Techniques: Picture yourself succeeding and achieving your goals.

5. Support Networks: Seek out friends, family, or mentors who can provide encouragement and support.

#1 Piece of Advice

My biggest advice is to prioritize self-care activities such as exercise, healthy eating, and proper sleep. Taking care of your physical and mental well-being can profoundly impact your mindset and attitude. When you try to care for yourself, you'll have more clarity, motivation, and resilience to overcome challenges. By investing in your well-being, you can build a solid foundation for self-confidence and success in the future.

Reflection Questions:

1. How has neglecting self-care affected your performance?
2. What aspects of self-care do you find most challenging?
3. Which self-care practices bring you the most benefit?
4. How can you better prioritize your well-being?
5. What support do you need to maintain self-care habits?

Chapter Summary

▶ Prioritize self-care activities like exercise, healthy eating, and proper sleep.

▶ Taking care of physical and mental well-being is essential for building confidence and overcoming self-doubt.

▶ Feeling better physically helps in tackling challenges and facing fears.

▶ Make self-care a daily routine to grow confidence and diminish self-doubt.

▶ Taking care of oneself is the first step towards realizing full potential.

It's important to prioritize self-care activities to maintain overall well-being. However, neglecting to seek help when needed can also have serious consequences on physical and mental health. In the following chapter, let's explore the mistake of not reaching out for assistance to ensure a comprehensive approach to self-care.

CHAPTER FIVE

NOT SEEKING HELP WHEN NEEDED

"Asking for help isn't a sign of weakness, it's a sign of wisdom." - Lori Deschene

Learning Objectives

After completing this chapter, you will be able to:

▶▶ Recognize when you need additional support or assistance

▶▶ Understand the value of seeking help in personal growth

- ▶ Identify appropriate resources for different types of challenges
- ▶ Develop strategies for effective communication with mentors and supporters
- ▶ Overcome common barriers to asking for help

Introduction

Jennifer sits alone in the school library, staring at her calculus homework. Despite spending hours studying, the concepts remain unclear, and her grades continue to decline. Her teacher offers after-school help sessions, and her friend suggests forming a study group, but Jennifer hesitates to accept either option. "I should be able to figure this out on my own," she thinks. Asking for help means I'm not smart enough."

This scenario illustrates a common struggle among students: the reluctance to seek help when facing challenges. This chapter explores why seeking support represents strength rather than weakness and provides strategies for building effective support networks.

Why Not Seeking Help When Needed is a Mistake

Not seeking help stems from the belief that asking for help is a sign of weakness or incompetence. This mistaken belief can prevent students from reaching out for support, even when they are struggling. In reality, seeking help shows strength, courage, and a willingness to learn and grow.

Fear of Judgment

One reason middle and high school students who are pessimistic and feel like failures make this mistake is the fear of judgment. Many students worry that seeking help will make them appear incapable or inadequate in the eyes of others, which can paralyze them from seeking the support they desperately need.

Lack of Trust

Another reason for this mistake is a lack of trust in adults or professionals. Some students may feel that adults or professionals will not understand their struggles or be able to help them. This lack of trust can lead to isolation and hopelessness as students struggle to navigate their challenges alone.

Feeling Overwhelmed

Finally, students may make this mistake when they feel overwhelmed or defeated. When faced with persistent feelings of failure and pessimism, students may convince themselves that no amount of help will make a difference. This defeatist attitude can prevent them from seeking the support and guidance that could help them overcome their challenges.

The Importance of Seeking Help

Students should seek help as soon as they feel overwhelmed, doubtful, or pessimistic. It is never too early to seek support, and doing so can prevent negative thinking from spiraling out of control.

Gaining Perspective

Students can gain valuable perspectives on their struggles by seeking help. Trusted adults and professionals can provide insights and advice that students may not have considered, helping them see their situation in a new light.

Learning Coping Strategies

Trusted adults and professionals can also teach students effective coping strategies for managing stress, overcoming self-doubt, and building resilience. These strategies can empower students to handle future challenges with greater confidence and success.

Building Resilience

Reaching out for help can also help students build resilience. By seeking support and learning to navigate their struggles, students can develop the skills and mindset needed to overcome setbacks and continue moving forward.

Practical Steps to Implement This Mindset

1. Identify Trusted Adults: Identify the adults or professionals you trust and respect in your life. This could be a teacher, coach, family member, or counselor.

2. Schedule a Meeting: Schedule a time to speak with them about your feelings of pessimism and failure. Be honest about your struggles and ask for their guidance and support.

3. Be Open and Honest: During your conversation, be open and honest about your feelings and experiences. This will help the person you are speaking with to understand your situation and provide the best possible advice and support.

4. Follow Through: Follow through on the advice and guidance you receive. Take the steps suggested to address your challenges and build confidence and resilience.

Overcoming Past Mistakes

If you've already made the mistake of not seeking help when needed, it's important to recognize that it's never too late to turn things around. Here are steps to overcome this habit:

1. Reach Out Now: Identify a trusted adult or professional and contact them immediately. Explain that you have been struggling and would like their support and guidance.

2. Develop a Support Network: Build a network of trusted individuals to whom you can turn for support in the future. This can include teachers, counselors, family members, and friends.

3. Practice Open Communication: Make a habit of communicating openly and honestly about your struggles. This will help you build stronger relationships and ensure you have the support you need when challenges arise.

4. Seek Professional Help if Needed: If you struggle with persistent feelings of failure and pessimism, consider seeking help from a mental health professional. They can provide specialized support and strategies to help you overcome these feelings.

Preventing Future Mistakes

To prevent the mistake of not seeking help in the future, commit to reaching out for support whenever you feel overwhelmed or doubtful. Recognize that seeking help is a sign of strength and that asking for support when needed is okay.

Tools to Help You Succeed

Several tools can help you prioritize seeking help and building confidence:

1. Cognitive Behavioral Therapy (CBT) is a talk therapy that helps you identify negative thought patterns and replace them with more positive and realistic thoughts. It can also help you challenge your pessimistic beliefs and develop a more optimistic outlook.

2. Mindfulness Meditation: Mindfulness meditation teaches you to be present in the moment and accept your thoughts and feelings without judgment. It can help you let go of negative self-talk and cultivate a greater self-compassion.

3. Goal setting: Setting realistic and achievable goals can help you regain control and purpose in your life. By breaking down larger

goals into smaller, manageable steps, you can build confidence in your ability to succeed.

4. Positive Affirmations: Repeating positive affirmations to yourself daily can help rewire your brain to focus on your strengths and potential rather than your perceived failures.

5. Support Networks: Seek out friends, family, or mentors who can provide encouragement and support. Having someone to talk to can make a world of difference.

#1 Piece of Advice

Here's my biggest advice if you feel like a failure and struggle with self-doubt: Contact trusted adults or professionals for support and guidance instead of internalizing your negative thoughts and feelings. This is incredibly important because navigating these feelings alone can often lead to a spiral of negativity, which can be challenging to overcome.

When you seek help, you're taking the first step toward overcoming self-doubt and building confidence in the future. Talking to someone you trust or seeking professional guidance can give you the tools and resources to work through your feelings and develop a more positive and hopeful mindset. You deserve to feel confident and supported, and by seeking help, you're allowing yourself to create a brighter and more fulfilling future.

I encourage you to take action on what you've learned in this chapter. Don't be afraid to reach out to a teacher, school counselor, or mental health professional if you're struggling with self-doubt and feelings of failure. By seeking support, you're demonstrating strength and resilience and taking an important step toward building a brighter and more confident future for yourself. You deserve to feel successful and fulfilled, and by seeking help, you're moving in the right direction.

Reflection Questions:

1. What prevents you from seeking help when needed?

2. How has receiving support benefited you in the past?

3. Which resources could you utilize more effectively?

4. How might helping others enhance your own growth?

5. What would change if you viewed seeking help as a strength?

Chapter Summary

▶ Reach out to trusted adults or professionals for support and guidance.

▶ Opening up about your struggles can provide valuable perspectives, advice, and tools.

▶ Remember, you are not alone in your journey.

▶ Embrace the opportunity to seek support and empower yourself.

▶ Overcome pessimism and failure with help from others.

As you navigate challenging situations, it's crucial to seek support from trusted adults or professionals. However, it's equally important to address the harmful effects of engaging in negative self-talk and thoughts, which we will explore in the following chapter. Please keep reading to discover the power of positive self-talk and its impact on your well-being.

CHAPTER SIX

ENGAGING IN NEGATIVE SELF-TALK AND THOUGHTS

"The way you speak to yourself matters. Your inner voice shapes your outer reality." - Michelle Obama

Learning Objectives

▶▶ After completing this chapter, you will be able to:

▶▶ Identify patterns of negative self-talk in your daily life

- ⏩ Understand the impact of internal dialogue on personal growth
- ⏩ Develop strategies for transforming negative thoughts into constructive ones
- ⏩ Implement techniques for building self-compassion
- ⏩ Create habits that support positive self-dialogue

Introduction

Thomas sits at his desk after receiving feedback on his English essay. Despite earning a B+, his mind fixates on constructive criticism. "I'm terrible at writing," he tells himself. "Everyone else probably did better. I'll never improve." This internal monologue represents a common challenge among students: the habit of negative self-talk that undermines confidence and hinders growth.

Negative self-talk acts as an internal critic, often speaking more harshly than any external voice would dare. This chapter explores how to recognize, challenge, and transform these internal messages into supportive dialogue that encourages growth and resilience.

Why Engaging in Negative Self-Talk is a Mistake

Engaging in negative self-talk and thoughts perpetuates a cycle of low self-esteem and self-doubt. When you constantly tell yourself you're not good enough and will never succeed, you start believing it. This can hold you back from taking risks, pursuing your goals, and achieving success.

External Influences

External factors, such as peer pressure, societal expectations, or academic stress, can influence students and lead to self-doubt and negative self-talk.

Fixed Mindset

A fixed mindset, the belief that abilities and intelligence are static, can lead to helplessness and a lack of motivation, resulting in negative self-talk and thoughts.

Past Failures

Experiences of failure or setbacks can cause students to doubt themselves, creating a negative mindset that is difficult to overcome.

When Students Make This Mistake

Students tend to engage in negative self-talk when faced with challenges, receive criticism, or compare themselves to others. It's easy to fall into the trap of negative thinking when things aren't going well, but it's important to recognize when this is happening and take steps to overcome it.

The Importance of Positive Self-Talk

Instead of engaging in negative self-talk and thoughts, practice self-compassion and speak to yourself with kindness. Challenge negative thoughts with positive affirmations and remind yourself of your strengths and abilities. Developing a growth mindset, seeking positive influences, and celebrating progress can also help overcome self-doubt and build confidence.

Building Confidence

Positive self-talk can significantly boost your confidence. By affirming your strengths and potential, you create a more positive self-image and increase your belief in your abilities.

Overcoming Challenges

Practicing self-compassion and using positive affirmations help you approach challenges with a more resilient and optimistic mindset. This shift in perspective can make overcoming obstacles and achieving your goals easier.

Practical Steps to Implement This Mindset

1. Monitor Your Inner Dialogue: Pay attention to your inner dialogue. Stop and replace those thoughts with kind and encouraging words when you catch yourself engaging in negative self-talk.

2. Practice Self-Compassion: Treat yourself as you would a friend going through a tough time. Be understanding and forgiving of your mistakes and shortcomings.

3. Use Positive Affirmations: Create a list of positive affirmations that resonate with you. Repeat these affirmations daily to reinforce a positive mindset.

4. Celebrate Small Victories: Acknowledge and celebrate your achievements, no matter how small. This practice helps build momentum and confidence.

Overcoming Past Mistakes

If you've already made the mistake of engaging in negative self-talk, you must recognize that you can turn things around. Here are steps to overcome this habit:

1. Seek Support: Talk to a mentor, teacher, or counselor who can provide guidance and encouragement.

2. Surround Yourself with Positivity: Seek out friends and peers who are positive and supportive. Avoid those who bring you down or contribute to your negative self-talk.

3. Set Realistic Goals: Focus on setting achievable goals and celebrating your progress. This will help build confidence and a sense of accomplishment.

4. Step Out of Your Comfort Zone: Take on new challenges to prove your capability and resilience.

Preventing Future Mistakes

To prevent negative self-talk in the future, practice self-compassion, speak to yourself with kindness, and challenge negative thoughts with positive affirmations. Recognize that everyone makes mistakes and that failure is a part of learning and growth. Focus on your accomplishments and progress, and surround yourself with supportive and positive people.

Tools to Help You Succeed

Several tools can help you prioritize positive self-talk and build confidence:

1. Journaling: Write down your thoughts and feelings in a journal. Writing down your negative thoughts can help you challenge them and reframe them into positive affirmations.

2. Mindfulness Practices: Mindfulness meditation and other relaxation techniques can help you become more aware of your negative thoughts and learn to address them with self-compassion.

3. Gratitude Exercises: Daily gratitude exercises can help you focus on the positive aspects of your life and combat pessimism and self-doubt.

4. Positive Affirmation Cards: Create or use positive affirmation cards to remind yourself of your strengths and potential.

5. Supportive Community: Seek out a supportive community of peers, mentors, or counselors who can encourage and provide positive reinforcement.

Real-Life Example of Overcoming Negative Self-Talk

Meet Sarah: A Journey to Self-Compassion

Sarah, who struggled with negative self-talk about her math abilities, decided to take action to change her mindset.

1. Recognizing Negative Thoughts:

Scenario: After receiving another low math grade, Sarah caught herself thinking, "I'm terrible at this."

Challenge: She questioned this thought, asking herself, "Is it true that I'm terrible at math, or do I just need more practice and help?"

2. Reframing and Positive Affirmations:

Reframe: Sarah started to reframe her thoughts. Instead of saying, "I'm terrible at math," she told herself, "I can improve with practice and help."

Affirmations: She began using positive affirmations daily, such as, "I am capable of learning and getting better at math."

3. Seeking Support and Practicing Self-Compassion:

Support: Sarah talked to her math teacher about her struggles and received additional help and resources.

Self-Compassion: She practiced self-compassion, reminding herself that struggling with a subject doesn't define her worth and that she is still valuable and capable.

4. Improved Mindset and Performance:

Outcome: Over time, Sarah's mindset shifted. She became more confident in her abilities and saw improvement in her math grades.

Growth: By addressing her negative self-talk, Sarah learned to approach challenges positively and resiliently.

#1 Piece of Advice

Here's my biggest advice on overcoming self-doubt and building confidence in the future: practice self-compassion, speak to yourself with kindness, and challenge negative thoughts with positive affirmations. As a middle or high school student, you are still growing and learning, and it's expected to experience self-doubt and feelings of failure. However, how you talk to yourself and the thoughts you entertain greatly impact your confidence and self-esteem.

Self-compassion allows you to be kind and understanding to yourself, especially during tough times. Speaking to yourself with kindness means using positive and encouraging language when you talk to yourself. Challenging negative thoughts with positive affirmations involves replacing negative thoughts with positive, empowering statements about yourself and your abilities.

Acting on this advice will help you overcome self-doubt and lay the foundation for a more positive, confident mindset in the future. By practicing self-compassion, speaking kindly to yourself, and using positive affirmations, you can cultivate a more resilient and confident attitude that will serve you academically and personally. Remember, you can shape your mindset and build your confidence to succeed.

Reflection Questions:

1. How does your internal dialogue affect your actions?
2. Which thought patterns most frequently challenge you?
3. What would change if you treated yourself with more compassion?
4. How can you support others in developing positive self-talk?
5. What positive affirmations resonate most strongly with you?

Chapter Summary

▶ Practice self-compassion and speak to yourself with kindness.

▶ Challenge negative thoughts with positive affirmations.

▶ Recognize that everyone makes mistakes and failure is part of learning and growth.

▶ Surround yourself with supportive and positive people.

▶ Set realistic goals and celebrate achievements, no matter how small.

As we learn to be kinder to ourselves, we must also be mindful of overthinking. Overthinking can hinder our progress and lead to unnecessary stress. In the next chapter, we will explore the impact of overthinking and strategies to overcome this common mistake, helping us cultivate a more balanced and compassionate mindset. Keep reading to discover the power of letting go and finding peace in the present moment.

CHAPTER SEVEN
OVERTHINKING

"The more you overthink, the less you will understand." - Habeeb Akande

Learning Objectives

After completing this chapter, you will be able to:

- ▶ Recognize signs of overthinking in your daily life
- ▶ Understand the difference between productive analysis and unhelpful rumination
- ▶ Develop strategies for managing excessive thoughts
- ▶ Implement techniques for staying present and focused

▶ Create habits that support balanced thinking patterns

Introduction

Emily stares at her phone, analyzing a text message from her friend for the third hour. "Maybe she's upset with me," she thinks, reviewing every interaction from the past week. "Does 'okay' with a period mean she's angry? Should I have said something different at lunch yesterday?" Meanwhile, her homework remains untouched, and her anxiety continues to build.

Overthinking transforms simple situations into complex problems, consuming mental energy and preventing productive action. This chapter explores recognizing when analytical thinking becomes counterproductive and developing strategies for maintaining a balanced perspective.

Why Overthinking is a Mistake

Overthinking keeps you in a cycle of negative thoughts and prevents you from taking positive action to improve your situation. When you overthink, you meditate on past mistakes and worry excessively about the future, which only fuels your feelings of failure and hopelessness. This can lead to a downward spiral of self-doubt and anxiety, making it even more challenging to break free from your negative mindset.

Recognizing Negative Thought Patterns

Firstly, many students may not have developed the skills to recognize and challenge negative thought patterns. Without these skills, it's easy to fall into the habit of overanalyzing every situation, which can exacerbate feelings of inadequacy and failure.

Academic and Social Pressures

Secondly, students may feel overwhelmed by academic and social pressures, leading them to analyze their past mistakes and worry about their future obsessively. This constant pressure can create a fertile ground for overthinking.

Lack of Support System

Finally, students may lack a support system of mentors or peers who can encourage them to practice mindfulness and shift their focus to the present moment. Without this support, breaking free from the habit of overthinking is challenging.

When Students Tend to Overthink

Students tend to overthink in times of stress and uncertainty, such as before an important test or when facing challenges in their personal lives. They may find themselves unable to stop dwelling on past failures or worrying about what could go wrong in the future, which can greatly impact their ability to concentrate and perform at their best.

The Importance of Mindfulness

Students struggling with feelings of failure and pessimism should practice mindfulness and focus on living in the present moment instead of overthinking. Mindfulness involves paying attention to your thoughts and feelings without judgment and redirecting your focus to the present rather than getting caught up in past or future concerns. This can be accomplished through practices such as meditation, deep breathing exercises, and grounding techniques that help you center yourself in the here and now.

Benefits of Mindfulness

Practicing mindfulness helps you recognize when overthinking and gently guides your thoughts back to the present. This can alleviate feelings of failure and self-doubt, reduce anxiety, and improve mental clarity. It also allows you to cultivate a more positive and balanced mindset, enabling you to approach challenges with greater resilience and confidence.

Practical Steps to Implement Mindfulness

1. Daily Meditation: Set aside a few minutes daily to sit quietly and focus on your breath. This simple practice can help calm your mind and reduce the tendency to overthink.

2. Deep Breathing Exercises: When you find yourself overthinking, take a few deep breaths and focus on the sensation of your breath entering and leaving your body. This can help ground you in the present moment.

3. Gratitude Journaling: Start a daily gratitude journal where you write down things you are thankful for. This practice shifts your focus from negative thoughts to positive aspects of your life.

4. Positive Affirmations: Create a list of positive affirmations that resonate with you. Repeat these affirmations daily to reinforce a positive mindset and counteract negative thoughts.

Overcoming Past Mistakes

If you've already made the mistake of overthinking, it's important to recognize that you can turn things around. Here are steps to overcome this habit:

1. Practice Gratitude: Focusing on what you are grateful for can shift your perspective and reduce the tendency to overthink.

2. Set Achievable Goals: Break down your larger goals into smaller, manageable tasks. This will help you focus on the present and reduce your tendency to worry about the future.

3. Surround Yourself with Positive Influences: Seek out friends and mentors who support and encourage you. A strong support system can help you stay focused on the present and overcome self-doubt.

4. Celebrate Your Successes: When you achieve a goal, no matter how small, take the time to acknowledge and celebrate your accomplishment. This boosts your confidence and reinforces a positive mindset.

Preventing Future Mistakes

To prevent overthinking in the future, practice mindfulness and live in the present moment. When you feel pessimistic or like a failure, take a moment to ground yourself in the present. Focus on what you can do right now to improve your situation rather than dwelling on past mistakes or worrying about the future. Mindfulness allows you to take control of your thoughts and emotions, helping you overcome self-doubt and build confidence.

Tools to Help You Succeed

Several tools can help you prioritize mindfulness and build confidence:

1. Meditation Apps: Use apps like Headspace or Calm to guide you through daily meditation practices.

2. Breathing Exercises: Practice breathing exercises to calm your mind and reduce anxiety.

3. Gratitude Journaling: Keep a gratitude journal to focus on the positive aspects of your life.

4. Positive Affirmation Cards: Create or use positive affirmation cards to remind yourself of your strengths and potential.

5. Support Networks: Seek out friends, family, or mentors who can provide encouragement and support.

Real-Life Examples of Overthinking

Overthinking can significantly hinder personal growth and success, especially for middle and high school students. It often involves dwelling on negative thoughts, worrying excessively about future events, and getting stuck in indecision and doubt. Here are some real-life examples of overthinking and its impact on student's lives:

Example 1: Exam Anxiety

Scenario:

John is a high school student who has always been an excellent academic performer. However, he often finds himself overthinking before exams. He worries about not remembering all the material, fears that he might misread the questions, and is anxious about what his parents and teachers will think if he doesn't score well.

Consequences:

Procrastination: John's overthinking leads him to procrastinate studying because he is so anxious about not doing well.

Performance Anxiety: On the day of the exam, John's anxiety peaks, and he finds it hard to focus. His mind goes blank during the test, and he does not perform as well as he could have.

Self-Doubt: After the exam, he keeps replaying every answer in his mind, doubting his choices and convincing himself that he did terribly, which impacts his confidence for future exams.

Example 2: Social Situations

Scenario:

Emily is a middle school student who overthinks social interactions. She constantly worries about saying the wrong thing or being judged by her peers. Before any social event, she goes through numerous potential conversations and outcomes in her head, trying to prepare for every possible scenario.

Consequences:

Avoidance: Emily starts avoiding social events because the thought of everything that could go wrong is too overwhelming.

Isolation: Her avoidance leads to isolation, making it harder for her to form meaningful friendships.

Increased Anxiety: When she does attend social events, her anxiety is so high that she struggles to be herself, which reinforces her fear of social interactions.

Example 3: Sports Performance

Scenario:

Mike is a talented player on his school's soccer team. However, he tends to overthink during games. He worries about making mistakes, letting his team down, and what the coach will think of his performance.

Consequences:

Hesitation: Mike's overthinking makes him hesitate during crucial moments in the game, causing him to miss opportunities to score or defend.

Decreased Enjoyment: The constant worry and self-criticism make the game less enjoyable for him, turning what should be a fun activity into a stressful ordeal.

Performance Decline: His performance starts to decline because he's so focused on not making mistakes that he forgets to play instinctively and confidently.

Example 4: Future Planning

Scenario:

Sophia is a high-achieving junior high school student starting to think about college. She overthinks every decision related to her future, from which colleges to apply to, what significance to choose, and how her choices will impact her career and life.

Consequences:

Paralysis by Analysis: Sophia spends so much time analyzing and overanalyzing every possible outcome that she struggles to make any decisions.

Missed Deadlines: Her inability to make decisions leads to missed application deadlines and opportunities.

Stress and Burnout: Sophia's constant worrying and overthinking cause significant stress and burnout, affecting her academic performance and mental health.

How to Overcome Overthinking

Overcoming overthinking involves several strategies that can help students break the cycle of worry and indecision:

1. Mindfulness and Meditation:

Practice: Engage in mindfulness exercises and meditation to help calm the mind and focus on the present moment.

Benefits: These practices can reduce anxiety and help students become more aware of their thoughts without getting caught up in them.

2. Setting Realistic Goals:

Small Steps: Break down large tasks into smaller, manageable steps to avoid feeling overwhelmed.

Focus: Concentrate on achieving one step at a time, which can reduce the tendency to overthink the entire process.

3. Positive Affirmations:

Encouragement: Use positive affirmations to build confidence and reduce negative self-talk.

Reinforcement: Regularly remind yourself of your strengths and past successes to counteract overthinking.

4. Seeking Support:

Talk to Someone: Share your worries with a trusted friend, family member, or counselor who can provide perspective and support.

Community: Surround yourself with positive influences who can help you stay grounded and focused.

5. Limit Information Overload:

Filter Information: Be selective about the information you consume, especially related to decisions and future planning.

Simplify Choices: Simplify your choices to avoid becoming overwhelmed by too many options.

#1 Piece of Advice

My biggest advice for middle and high school students feeling pessimistic and like a failure is to practice mindfulness and live in the present moment. Getting caught up in negative thoughts about the future is easy, but focusing on the present can overcome self-doubt and build confidence.

Mindfulness is being fully present and aware of your thoughts, feelings, and surroundings. By practicing mindfulness, you can become more aware of negative thought patterns and learn to redirect them positively. This can help you overcome feelings of failure and pessimism and build confidence in your ability to succeed in the future.

Practicing mindfulness is important because it can help you break free from the cycle of negative thinking and self-doubt. By focusing on the present moment, you can learn to appreciate what you have and become more aware of your opportunities. This can help you build the confidence to overcome obstacles and achieve your goals.

I encourage you to take action on what you've learned in this chapter by spending a few minutes each day practicing mindfulness. You can start by simply taking a few deep breaths and focusing on your body's sensations. Over time, you can incorporate mindfulness practices into your daily routine and watch as your self-doubt diminishes and your confidence grows. Remember, the present moment is the only moment we truly have, and by living mindfully, you can learn to overcome pessimism and build a brighter future for yourself.

Reflection Questions:

1. How does overthinking affect your daily life?
2. Which situations trigger excessive analysis?
3. What strategies help you return to the present moment?
4. How might limiting overthinking benefit your relationships?
5. What would change if you committed to action over analysis?

Chapter Summary

▶ Practice mindfulness and live in the present moment.

▶ Ground yourself in the present when feeling pessimistic or like a failure.

▶ Focus on improving your current situation instead of dwelling on the past or worrying about the future.

▶ Mindfulness can help overcome self-doubt and build confidence.

▶ Learn to quiet negative voices and focus on the positive aspects of life.

Overthinking can significantly impact a student's life, leading to anxiety, procrastination, and missed opportunities. By recognizing the patterns of overthinking and implementing strategies to manage it, students can break free from the cycle of worry and indecision. This shift can lead to improved performance, better mental health, and a more positive and confident approach to life.

Now that we've discussed the importance of living in the present moment, we must address the common mistake of allowing fear to hold us back from our true potential. By understanding how fear can limit us, we can work towards overcoming it and achieving our goals. Keep reading to learn how to conquer your fears and take control of your future.

CHAPTER EIGHT

ALLOWING FEAR TO HOLD YOU BACK

"Fear is not meant to stop you. It is meant to make you pause, plan, and proceed with greater awareness." - Unknown

Learning Objectives

After completing this chapter, you will be able to:

▶ Identify different types of fear and their impact on personal growth

▶ Understand the difference between protective and limiting fears

▶▶ Develop strategies for confronting and managing fears

▶▶ Implement techniques for building courage

▶▶ Create action plans that support moving forward despite fears

Introduction

Samuel stands backstage at the school talent show, his heart racing. For months, he has practiced his guitar performance, receiving encouragement from his music teacher and family. Yet, as the moment approaches to take the stage, fear threatens to overwhelm him. "What if I make a mistake? What if everyone laughs? Maybe I should go home." His hands shake as he contemplates walking away from an opportunity he has dreamed about for years.

Fear is a natural protective mechanism, but when we allow it to dictate our choices, it becomes a barrier to growth and achievement. This chapter explores recognizing when fear holds us back and developing the courage to move forward despite our anxieties.

Why Allowing Fear to Hold You Back is a Mistake

Allowing fear to dictate your actions prevents you from reaching your full potential and experiencing life's many opportunities. By letting fear control you, you limit yourself and miss out on valuable experiences and personal growth.

Fixed Mindset

Firstly, students may have a fixed mindset, believing their abilities and intelligence are set in stone. This can lead to a fear of taking risks and stepping out of their comfort zone, as they may believe that failure is inevitable.

Past Failures

Secondly, students may have experienced past failures or setbacks that have reinforced their negative beliefs about themselves, further fueling their fear of taking risks.

Societal Pressures

Lastly, societal pressures and comparisons to their peers can also contribute to their lack of confidence and fear of failure.

When Students Make This Mistake

Students tend to make the mistake of allowing fear to hold them back when faced with challenges or opportunities for growth. Whether trying out for a sports team, speaking up in class, or pursuing a new passion, their fear can prevent them from taking the necessary steps to achieve their goals and fulfill their potential.

The Importance of Confronting Fears and Taking Risks

Instead of allowing fear to hold them back, students should focus on building their confidence and overcoming self-doubt. This can be achieved through various strategies, such as setting small, achievable goals, seeking mentors and role models, and reframing their negative beliefs about themselves. By confronting their fears and taking risks, they can develop resilience and a growth mindset, ultimately paving the way for success and personal fulfillment.

Building Confidence

Taking risks and confronting fears helps build confidence. Each time you step out of your comfort zone and succeed, you reinforce the belief that you are capable and resilient.

Personal Growth

By facing challenges head-on, you open yourself up to new experiences and opportunities for personal growth. This helps you build confidence and prepares you to handle future challenges with greater ease.

Practical Steps to Confront Fears

1. Identify Your Fears: Identify the fears and doubts holding you back. Write them down and reflect on how they impact your actions and decisions.

2. Set Achievable Goals: Break down your larger goals into smaller, manageable steps. This will make it easier to take the first step and build momentum as you achieve each small goal.

3. Seek Support: Reach out to trusted adults, mentors, or peers who can provide guidance and encouragement. Their support can help you feel more confident in taking risks.

4. Reframe Negative Thoughts: Challenge negative beliefs about yourself and reframe them more positively. For example, instead of thinking, "I will fail," remind yourself, "Failure is a part of learning and growing."

Overcoming Past Mistakes

If you've already allowed fear to hold you back, it's important to recognize that it's never too late to turn things around. Here are steps to overcome this habit:

1. Join New Activities: Participate in clubs, sports, or extracurricular activities that interest you. This helps you build confidence and meet new people.

2. Take on Leadership Roles: Volunteer for leadership positions in school projects or community organizations. This challenges you to step up and develop new skills.

3. Find a Mentor: Seek a mentor who can guide and support you as you work to overcome your fears.

4. Celebrate Small Victories: Acknowledge and celebrate your achievements, no matter how small. This reinforces positive behavior and builds confidence.

Preventing Future Mistakes

Commit to confronting your fears and taking risks to prevent fear from holding you back in the future. Recognize that failure is a natural part of learning and growth and that taking risks is essential for personal and academic success.

Tools to Help You Succeed

Several tools can help you confront your fears and build confidence:

1. Mindfulness and Meditation: Practice mindfulness and meditation to manage negative thoughts and emotions and improve self-awareness and focus.

2. Positive Self-Talk: Use positive affirmations and self-encouragement to rewire your mindset and build self-confidence.

3. Goal Setting: Set realistic and achievable goals to give you a sense of direction and purpose and help you feel accomplished.

4. Seeking Support: Surround yourself with positive and supportive people who can provide encouragement and guidance.

5. Personal Development Resources: Utilize self-help books, podcasts, and online courses to gain knowledge and skills to increase your confidence and help you overcome self-doubt.

#1 Piece of Advice

My biggest advice on overcoming self-doubt and building confidence is to confront your fears and take risks. It's natural to feel uncertain and afraid of failure, but allowing these feelings to paralyze you will only hinder your potential for success.

Confronting your fears and taking risks is essential because it allows you to break free from the cycle of negative thinking and self-doubt. Taking risks means stepping out of your comfort zone and opening yourself up to new opportunities and experiences. This can lead to personal growth, increased self-confidence, and a deeper understanding of your capabilities and potential.

I encourage you to act on what you've learned in this chapter. Start by identifying the fears and doubts that are holding you back and make a conscious effort to confront them. Push yourself to take calculated risks, whether trying out for a sports team, raising your hand in class, or pursuing a new hobby. Each small risk you take will build your confidence and resilience, ultimately leading to a more positive outlook on your abilities and future. Remember, it's okay to feel afraid, but don't let it stop you from reaching your full potential. You have the power to overcome self-doubt and build confidence in the future.

Reflection Questions:

1. How has fear influenced your choices?
2. Which types of fear impact you most significantly?
3. What opportunities have you missed due to fear?
4. How might your life change with more courage?
5. What support do you need to face your fears?

Chapter Summary

- ▶ Confront fears and take risks.

- ▶ Overcome self-doubt and build confidence.

- ▶ It's okay to fail; get back up and keep pushing forward.

- ▶ Believe in yourself and take risks.

- ▶ Achieve the unknown.

As you bravely confront your fears and take risks, it's important to set clear boundaries for yourself and others. In the following chapter, we will explore the mistake of not setting boundaries and the impact it can have on your personal and professional relationships. Understanding the importance of this topic is crucial for continuing to grow and thrive. Keep reading to learn valuable insights on this essential aspect of self-care.

CHAPTER NINE

NOT SETTING BOUNDARIES

"Boundaries are the lines we draw that mark the edges of who we are. They protect our time, energy, and sense of self." - Brené Brown

Learning Objectives

After completing this chapter, you will be able to:

- ▶▶ Understand the fundamental importance of personal boundaries
- ▶▶ Recognize situations that require boundary-setting

▶ Develop effective strategies for establishing boundaries

▶ Implement techniques for maintaining boundaries respectfully

▶ Create systems for protecting your time and energy

Introduction

Amanda excels academically and participates in numerous extracurricular activities. When classmates repeatedly ask her to complete their assignments, she agrees despite her overwhelming schedule. Her desire to help others and fear of disappointing them make her sacrifice her well-being. As a result, her grades begin to slip, her stress levels increase, and her passion for learning diminishes.

Setting and maintaining healthy boundaries is fundamental to personal well-being and sustainable success. This chapter explores how to establish appropriate limits while maintaining positive relationships and achieving goals.

Why Not Setting Boundaries is a Mistake

Not setting boundaries can be a huge mistake for these students. Firstly, it can lead to feelings of burnout and overwhelm. When you don't set boundaries, you're constantly saying yes to everything and everyone, which can leave you exhausted and drained. This can further contribute to feelings of failure and pessimism as you struggle to keep up with all your time and energy demands.

Burnout and Overwhelm

Without boundaries, you may be overcommitting to various activities and obligations, leading to burnout. This exhaustion can negatively impact your academic performance and personal well-being.

Neglecting Self-Care

Secondly, not setting boundaries can make prioritizing your well-being and mental health challenging. When you constantly say yes to others, you may neglect your needs and feel worse about yourself. This can lead to a downward spiral of self-doubt and lack of confidence.

Toxic Relationships

Lastly, not setting boundaries can result in toxic relationships and unhealthy dynamics. Without clear boundaries, it's easy for others to take advantage of you and put you in situations that are not in your best interest. This can further erode your self-esteem and make overcoming feelings of failure and pessimism even harder.

When Students Make This Mistake

Middle and high school students who are pessimistic and feel like failures tend to make this mistake when they are desperate to feel accepted and liked. They may fear rejection and believe that saying no will make them disliked or ostracized. This fear can drive them to people-please and strive to please others at their own expense.

The Importance of Setting Healthy Boundaries

Instead of allowing themselves to be overwhelmed and taken advantage of, these students should focus on establishing healthy boundaries in their relationships and activities. This means learning to say no when something doesn't align with their values or priorities and setting limits on their time and energy. It also means surrounding themselves with people who respect their boundaries and support their well-being.

Regaining Control

By establishing boundaries, students can regain control over their lives and build the confidence they need to overcome their feelings of failure and pessimism. This helps to create a more balanced and fulfilling lifestyle.

Building Self-Worth

Setting boundaries shows that you value yourself and your time. It helps build self-respect and self-worth, crucial for overcoming self-doubt and developing confidence.

Practical Steps to Implement Boundaries

1. Evaluate Your Commitments: Assess your current activities and relationships. Identify which ones are draining and which ones are fulfilling.

2. Learn to Say No: Practice saying no to commitments that do not serve your well-being or align with your goals.

3. Set Time Limits: Allocate specific times for activities and stick to them. This helps prevent overcommitment and ensures you have time for self-care.

4. Communicate Clearly: Be assertive and clear when setting boundaries with others. Explain your limits and the reasons behind them.

Overcoming Past Mistakes

If you've already made the mistake of not setting boundaries, it's important to recognize that it's never too late to change. Here are steps to overcome this habit:

1. Seek Support: Talk to a trusted adult, mentor, or counselor about your struggles with setting boundaries. They can offer guidance and support.

2. Practice Self-Care: Make self-care a priority. Schedule a regular time for activities that rejuvenate and fulfill you.

3. Reassess Relationships: Surround yourself with people who respect your boundaries and support your well-being.

4. Reflect on Progress: Regularly reflect on your progress in setting and maintaining boundaries. Adjust as needed to ensure they continue to serve you well.

Preventing Future Mistakes

Commit to prioritizing your well-being to prevent the mistake of not setting boundaries in the future. Recognize that setting boundaries is a form of self-respect and essential for maintaining a healthy and balanced life.

Tools to Help You Succeed

Several tools can help you establish and maintain healthy boundaries:

1. Boundary-Setting Books: Read books on setting boundaries to gain insights and strategies. Examples include "Boundaries" by Dr. Henry Cloud and Dr. John Townsend.

2. Time Management Apps: Use apps like Trello or Todoist to manage your commitments and ensure you have time for self-care.

3. Self-Care Routines: Develop a self-care routine that includes exercise, meditation, and hobbies.

4. Support Groups: Join support groups or online communities to share experiences and learn from others.

5. Therapy: Consider talking to a therapist to work through any underlying issues related to setting boundaries.

#1 Piece of Advice

Here's my most extensive advice on overcoming self-doubt and building confidence: Establish healthy boundaries in your relationships and activities. It is essential to recognize that your past mistakes or shortcomings do not determine your worth. By setting healthy boundaries, you can protect yourself from toxic influences and create a positive environment for personal growth. Surround yourself with supportive friends and mentors who uplift and encourage you, and engage in activities that bring you joy and fulfillment.

Establishing healthy boundaries is crucial for your mental and emotional well-being. It will help you build confidence and self-respect and empower you to focus on your strengths and aspirations. Don't be afraid to say no to people or activities that drain your energy and self-esteem. By prioritizing your well-being, you can create a positive mindset and overcome self-doubt.

Act on what you've learned in this chapter by reflecting on your current relationships and activities. Are there any that make you feel inadequate or bring negativity into your life? Make a conscious effort to set boundaries that protect your self-worth and promote personal growth. Surround yourself with positivity and encouragement, and believe in your ability to overcome challenges and achieve success.

Reflection Questions:

1. Where do you need stronger boundaries?
2. How have weak boundaries affected your well-being?
3. What challenges do you face in setting boundaries?

4. How might strong boundaries improve your life?

5. What support do you need to maintain boundaries?

Chapter Summary

▶ Establishing healthy boundaries is crucial for mental and emotional well-being.

▶ Surround yourself with people who uplift and support you.

▶ Engage in activities that bring you joy and fulfillment.

▶ Prioritize your well-being and happiness.

▶ Build confidence and prevent self-doubt by setting limits.

Establishing healthy boundaries is as important as being mindful of the influences we surround ourselves with. In the following chapter, we will explore the mistake of surrounding ourselves with negative influences and the impact it can have on our relationships and well-being. Stay tuned to discover how to navigate this common pitfall and create a more positive and supportive environment.

CHAPTER TEN

SURROUNDING YOURSELVES WITH NEGATIVE INFLUENCES

"Negative people will always try to drag you down. Surround yourself with those who lift you up." Zig Ziglar

Learning Objectives

After completing this chapter, you will be able to:

▷ Recognize the impact of social influences on personal development

▷ Identify characteristics of positive and negative relationships

▷ Develop strategies for cultivating supportive friendships

▷ Implement techniques for managing challenging relationships

▷ Create environments that foster growth and success

Introduction

Olivia's grades began declining in her sophomore year, coinciding with a shift in her social circle. Her new friends regularly skipped classes, dismissed academic achievement, and ridiculed students who participated in school activities. Though she recognized the negative changes in her behavior and attitude, Olivia worried that distancing herself from these friends would leave her isolated. This internal conflict between personal growth and social acceptance represents a common challenge for many students.

Our social environment profoundly influences our mindset, decisions, and future opportunities. This chapter explores recognizing negative influences and creating relationships that support personal growth and achievement.

Why Surrounding Yourself with Negative Influences is a Mistake

Surrounding yourself with negative influences is a mistake because it reinforces your negative feelings and attitudes. If you're already feeling pessimistic and like a failure, being around people who share those feelings will only worsen things. Instead, seeking positive and supportive friendships can uplift you and help you see your potential.

Reinforcing Negative Beliefs

When you consistently engage with negative influences, you internalize their pessimism and self-doubt. This can deepen your feelings of inadequacy and failure, making it harder to break free from these destructive thought patterns.

Lowering Self-Esteem

Negative influences can erode self-esteem by constantly highlighting flaws and failures. They can also prevent people from seeing their strengths and achievements, leading to a cycle of self-criticism and low self-worth.

Hindering Personal Growth

Negative influences can discourage you from taking risks, trying new things, and pursuing your goals. This can stifle your personal growth and prevent you from reaching your full potential.

Why Students Make This Mistake

There are three reasons why middle and high school students who are pessimistic and feel like failures tend to make this mistake.

Feeling Undeserving

Feeling down on yourself can lead you to believe that negative influences are all you deserve. This mindset can trap you in unhealthy relationships and prevent you from seeking better connections.

Lack of Awareness

You may not realize the impact that negative influences are having on you. It's not always easy to see how your friends and peers affect your mindset, especially when you're already feeling low.

Fear of Rejection

You might feel like you don't have any other options. When you're feeling like a failure, it can be hard to imagine that there are better friendships out there waiting for you. The fear of rejection can drive you to stick with familiar but negative relationships.

When Students Make This Mistake

Students tend to surround themselves with negative influences when they are feeling the lowest. When you're already feeling pessimistic and like a failure, it's easy to seek out connections that reinforce those feelings rather than challenge them.

What to Do Instead

Seek Out Positive and Supportive Friendships

Look for people who uplift you, who help you see the good in yourself and the world around you. Surround yourself with people who believe in you and encourage you to be your best self. Positive and supportive friendships can inspire you to reach your full potential and provide a buffer against life's challenges.

Practical Steps to Find Positive Friendships

1. Join Clubs and Activities: Join clubs or extracurricular activities to meet like-minded individuals who share your interests and values.

2. Attend Community Events: Get involved in community events or volunteer work to connect with positive role models and mentors.

3. Be Open to New Friendships: Try to connect with new people and be willing to let go of toxic relationships that bring you down.

4. Seek Support Groups: Join support groups or counseling sessions to build a network of positive and supportive individuals.

Consequences of Surrounding Yourself with Negative Influences

The mistake of surrounding yourself with negative influences can have terrible, life-ruining consequences. It reinforces feelings of worthlessness, low self-esteem, and a lack of motivation. This negative mindset can shape your entire outlook on life, leading to missed opportunities and unfulfilled potential.

Missing Opportunities

Negative influences can discourage you from pursuing new opportunities, leading to a lack of personal and academic growth. This can have long-term effects on your future success and happiness.

Mental Health Impact

Constant exposure to negativity can take a toll on your mental health, leading to anxiety, depression, and other emotional issues. This can make breaking free from the cycle of negativity even harder.

Typical Solutions That Don't Work

Many middle and high school students who feel like failures try to overcome these struggles by seeking validation from others, comparing themselves to peers, or attempting to overachieve. However, these solutions fail to address the root cause of their pessimism and low self-esteem.

Seeking Validation

Seeking validation from others creates a dependency on external approval, reinforcing the belief that others determine your worth.

Comparing Yourself to Peers

Comparing yourself to others can perpetuate feelings of inadequacy, as you may always find someone who seems to be doing better than you.

Overachieving

Overachieving to prove your worth can lead to burnout and exhaustion, further damaging your self-esteem.

The Best Way to Avoid This Mistake

Instead, seek out positive and supportive friendships. The people you surround yourself with greatly impact your mindset and outlook on life. Positive and supportive friends will uplift, encourage, and help you see the good in yourself. They will challenge you to grow and push you to reach your full potential.

Real-World Examples

1. Joining a Sports Team: Join a sports team emphasizing teamwork and positive reinforcement.
2. Participating in School Clubs: Get involved in clubs focusing on positive activities, such as community service or creative arts.
3. Finding a Mentor: Seek a mentor who can guide and support your personal and academic life.
4. Engaging in Positive Online Communities: Join online communities that promote positivity and personal growth.

How to Fix the Mistake if You've Already Made It

If negative influences surround you and feel like a failure, it's not too late to turn things around. Here are steps to fix this mistake:

1. Join Positive Activities: Participate in clubs or organizations focusing on positive activities or community service.

2. Find a Mentor: Seek out a mentor or role model who can provide guidance and support.

3. Engage in Inspiring Activities: Participate in extracurricular activities that inspire and motivate you.

4. Build Positive Relationships: Seek positive relationships with teachers or other adults who can provide encouragement and guidance.

Preventing Future Mistakes

To prevent making this mistake in the future, intentionally seek out positive and supportive friendships. Surround yourself with friends who encourage and support you. These friendships will uplift and inspire you to strive for success and overcome obstacles.

Tools to Help You Succeed

Several tools can help you avoid negative influences and seek positive friendships:

1. Mindfulness and Meditation: Practice mindfulness and meditation to improve self-awareness and manage negative thoughts.

2. Positive Affirmations: Use positive affirmations to rewire your mindset and boost self-confidence.

3. Goal Setting: Set realistic and achievable goals to provide a sense of direction and accomplishment.

4. Support Groups: Join support groups or counseling sessions to build a network of positive influences.

5. Gratitude Journals: Keep a gratitude journal to shift focus from negativity to appreciation.

#1 Piece of Advice

Here's my most extensive advice: Instead of succumbing to pessimism and self-doubt, seek out positive and supportive friendships. Surrounding yourself with negative influences can only sustain feelings of failure and hopelessness. By seeking out positive and supportive friendships, you will be surrounded by people who uplift and encourage you rather than bring you down. These friends inspire you to take on new challenges, support you through tough times, and help you see your potential.

Reflection Questions:

1. How do your current relationships affect your goals?
2. Which relationships support your growth most effectively?
3. What changes would improve your social environment?
4. How can you contribute positively to others' growth?
5. What support do you need to maintain positive relationships?

Chapter Summary

▶ Seek positive and supportive friendships.

▶ Avoid negative influences.

▶ Surround yourself with friends who encourage and support you.

▶ Choose friends who have a positive outlook on life.

▶ The company you keep significantly impacts your mindset and future success.

As we have discussed the importance of seeking positive and supportive friendships, it is also crucial to recognize the role of gratitude in maintaining healthy relationships. In the bonus chapter, we will explore the mistake of lacking gratitude and its impact on our friendships and overall well-being. Gratitude is a cornerstone of meaningful connections, so I encourage you to keep reading to learn more about its significance.

CHAPTER ELEVEN

BONUS: LACK OF GRATITUDE

"Gratitude turns what we have into enough." - Melody Beattie

Learning Objectives

After completing this chapter, you will be able to:

▷ Understand the fundamental role of gratitude in personal development

▷ Recognize opportunities for expressing appreciation in daily life

⯈ Develop sustainable gratitude practices

⯈ Implement techniques for deepening appreciation

⯈ Create habits that foster lasting contentment

Introduction

I saved Gratitude for last because it is the cornerstone of Rise Above. Consider Katherine, who excelled academically and participated in numerous extracurricular activities, yet she constantly focused on what she lacked rather than what she had achieved. Despite earning excellent grades, she dwelled on the few missed points rather than celebrating her successes. When friends received recognition, she felt diminished rather than inspired. Her inability to appreciate her circumstances and achievements prevented her from experiencing genuine satisfaction and joy in her accomplishments.

Gratitude serves as a foundational element for personal growth and satisfaction. This chapter explores how developing appreciation enhances our experiences and relationships while creating a positive framework for future success.

Understanding Gratitude

Gratitude represents more than politeness or temporary appreciation. It encompasses a more profound recognition of value in our experiences, relationships, and opportunities. This perspective transforms how we view challenges and achievements while enhancing our capacity for joy and resilience.

Ignoring Problems

Gratitude should not be used to ignore or dismiss legitimate problems and challenges. Acknowledging and addressing issues while finding aspects of your life to appreciate is important.

Lack of Consistency

Practicing gratitude inconsistently can lead to minimal benefits. To be effective, gratitude should be a regular, intentional practice.

Why Students Make This Mistake

There are a few reasons why middle and high school students who are pessimistic and feel like failures struggle to practice gratitude effectively.

1. Influence of Peers: Teenagers are heavily influenced by their peers. It can be easy to fall into the same mindset if they are surrounded by negative influences that constantly reinforce pessimism and failure. This can include friends who continually complain or put others down or even social media influencers who promote a negative outlook on life.

2. Negative Self-Talk: Many students engage in negative self-talk, constantly putting themselves down and focusing on their perceived failures. This can lead to a lack of gratitude for the positive aspects of their lives as they become blinded by their negativity.

3. Pressure from School and Society: The pressures of school and society can also contribute to a lack of gratitude. Students are often under immense pressure to succeed academically and socially. When they feel like they are not meeting these expectations, it can be easy to become consumed by feelings of failure.

When Students Make This Mistake

Middle and high school students tend to make this mistake during times of high stress, such as exams, social events, or when facing challenges in their personal lives. These times make them more susceptible to the influence of negative people and thoughts, leading to a lack of gratitude for the positive aspects of their lives.

What to Do Instead

Practice Genuine Gratitude

Instead of surrounding themselves with negative influences and falling into a pattern of pessimism and feeling like a failure, students should practice genuine gratitude for the positive aspects of their lives. They should seek out positive influences, such as friends who uplift and support them or mentors who can provide guidance and encouragement. By practicing gratitude and focusing on the good things in their lives, students can shift their mindset towards a more positive and hopeful outlook.

Practical Steps to Cultivate Genuine Gratitude

1. Gratitude Journal: Keep a daily journal in which you write down three things you are genuinely grateful for. Reflect on why you are grateful for these things and how they positively impact your life.

2. Mindful Reflection: Spend a few minutes each day focusing on the positive aspects of your life. This can help you internalize feelings of gratitude and appreciation.

3. Express Gratitude to Others: Take the time to thank people who have positively impacted your life. Expressing gratitude to others can strengthen your relationships and enhance your own feelings of gratitude.

4. Positive Environment: Surround yourself with positive influences. Engage with friends, family members, and mentors who encourage and uplift you.

Consequences of Not Practicing Gratitude

Not practicing gratitude for the positive aspects of your life can lead to a downward spiral of negative thinking, poor self-esteem, and missed opportunities. When you constantly focus on the negative aspects of your life, you miss the chance to see the good things happening around you. This can lead to hopelessness and despair, making it difficult to see a path forward.

The consequences are much worse than you think. Surrounding yourself with negative influences can lead to a lack of motivation, poor academic performance, and a negative mindset that can follow you into adulthood. You might think that being pessimistic and feeling like a failure is just a phase you'll grow out of, but it can shape your entire outlook on life.

Typical Solutions That Don't Work

Many middle and high school students try these solutions when they feel pessimistic and like failures. However, surrounding yourself with negative influences is not a good fix for feeling like a failure. It only perpetuates the negative mindset and can lead to feelings of inadequacy and hopelessness. Seeking validation from others, comparing oneself to peers, or overachieving to prove worth do not address the root cause of their pessimism and low self-esteem.

The Best Way to Avoid This Mistake

Instead, practice gratitude for the positive aspects of your life. Surrounding yourself with negative influences will only reinforce the feelings of pessimism and failure. Practicing gratitude helps shift your focus from the negative to the positive. When you practice gratitude, you train your mind to see the good in every situation and appreciate your life's blessings. This positive mindset can help you overcome feelings of pessimism and failure.

Real-World Examples

1. Gratitude Jar: Create a gratitude jar where you write down things you are grateful for on small pieces of paper and place them in the jar. When you are feeling down, take a few out and remind yourself of the positive things in your life.

2. Positive social media: Follow social media accounts that promote positivity and inspiration. This can help counterbalance the negativity you may encounter online.

3. Volunteering: Engage in volunteer work or community service. Helping others can give you a sense of purpose and highlight the positive impact you can have on the world.

4. Positive Role Models: Seek positive role models and mentors who embody gratitude and a positive mindset. Surround yourself with their influence and learn from their example.

How to Fix the Mistake if You've Already Made It

It's not too late to turn things around if you've already made this mistake. Here are steps to fix this mistake:

1. Gratitude Practice: Start a gratitude journal and write down three things you are grateful for daily.

2. Positive Influences: Seek out positive role models and mentors who can provide guidance and support.

3. Express Gratitude: Take the time to thank people who have positively impacted your life.

4. Mindful Reflection: Spend a few minutes each day in mindful reflection, focusing on the positive aspects of your life.

Preventing Future Mistakes

To prevent making this mistake in the future, intentionally seek out positive and supportive friendships. Surround yourself with friends who encourage and support you. These friendships will uplift and inspire you to strive for success and overcome obstacles. Practicing gratitude for the positive aspects of your life can shift your mindset and help you see the world in a more positive light.

Tools to Help You Succeed

There are specific tools that middle and high school students who are pessimistic and like failures can use to prevent the mistake of surrounding themselves with negative influences in the future. Here are five specific tools to help you with this issue:

1. Gratitude Journal: Start each day by writing down three things you are grateful for. This will help you shift your focus from negativity to positivity.

2. Positive Affirmations: Write down and repeat positive statements about yourself and your abilities. This will help rewire your brain to think more positively.

3. Surround Yourself with Positive People: Seek out friends and mentors with a positive outlook on life. Their positive energy can help lift you up.

4. Limit social media and News Consumption: Take breaks from social media and limit your exposure to negative news. This can help prevent you from being surrounded by negativity.

5. Practice Mindfulness: Engage in mindfulness practice, such as meditation or deep breathing exercises. This can help you stay present and focused on the positive aspects of your life.

Real-Life Examples of Gratitude

Gratitude is a powerful tool that can transform our mindset and improve our overall well-being. Practicing gratitude helps us focus on the positive aspects of our lives, fostering a sense of contentment and happiness. Here are some real-life examples of how gratitude can make a significant difference in the lives of middle and high school students:

Example 1: Academic Stress Relief

Scenario:

Maria is a high school student who often feels overwhelmed by her academic workload. She struggles to stay positive and motivated between homework, projects, and extracurricular activities.

Practicing Gratitude:

Daily Gratitude Journal: Maria started keeping a gratitude journal, writing down three things she is grateful for daily. These can be simple things like a sunny day, a kind word from a teacher, or a fun moment with friends.

Shift in Perspective: As she continues this practice, Maria notices a change in her perspective. She begins to focus more on the positive aspects of her day, which helps reduce her stress and improve her overall mood.

Impact:

Improved Mental Health: Maria feels less anxious about her workload and more capable of handling her responsibilities.

Increased Motivation: Her focus on gratitude boosts her motivation to complete her tasks and strive for success.

Example 2: Enhancing Relationships

Scenario:

Jake is a middle school student who feels disconnected from his peers. He often worries about fitting in and struggles to make friends.

Practicing Gratitude:

Expressing Appreciation: Jake decides to express gratitude to his classmates and teachers. He starts by thanking a classmate who helps him with a difficult assignment and writing a thank-you note to his teacher.

Building Connections: By showing appreciation, Jake begins to build stronger connections with his peers. They respond positively to his gratitude, which helps him feel more included and valued.

Impact:

Improved Social Skills: Jake becomes more comfortable interacting with others and making new friends.

Enhanced Relationships: His relationships with classmates and teachers improve, creating a more supportive and positive school environment.

Example 3: Coping with Personal Challenges

Scenario:

Emma is a high school student who is facing personal challenges at home. Her parents are divorcing, and she feels overwhelmed by the changes in her family dynamics.

Practicing Gratitude:

Finding Silver Linings: To help cope with her feelings, Emma starts a gratitude practice. She looks for silver linings in her situation, such as the support from her friends or the quality time she gets to spend with each parent individually.

Gratitude Letters: She writes gratitude letters to her parents, expressing appreciation for their love and support despite the difficult circumstances.

Impact:

Emotional Resilience: Emma's focus on gratitude helps her develop emotional resilience, which allows her to cope better with her family's changes.

Positive Mindset: Her gratitude practice shifts her mindset from dwelling on the negatives to appreciating the positives in her life.

Example 4: Boosting Self-Esteem

Scenario:

Liam is a middle school student who struggles with low self-esteem. He often feels inadequate and compares himself to his peers, which affects his confidence.

Practicing Gratitude:

Gratitude for Self: Liam starts practicing gratitude for his own strengths and accomplishments. Each night, he writes down something he did well or something he likes about himself.

Positive Affirmations: He also incorporates positive affirmations into his daily routine, reminding himself of his worth and capabilities.

Impact:

Increased Self-Esteem: Liam's focus on his strengths helps boost his self-esteem and confidence.

Reduced Comparisons: By appreciating his unique qualities, Liam reduces the negative impact of comparing himself to others.

How to Cultivate Gratitude

Practicing gratitude can be integrated into daily life through simple and consistent actions:

1. Gratitude Journals:

Daily Entries: Write down three things you are grateful for each day. This practice helps shift your focus from negative thoughts to positive ones.

Reflective Writing: Reflect on the reasons behind your gratitude and how these positive aspects impact your life.

2. Gratitude Letters:

Expressing Appreciation: Write letters to people you appreciate, expressing your gratitude for their support and kindness.

Building Connections: Share these letters with the recipients to strengthen your relationships and foster a sense of connection.

3. Mindfulness Practices:

Being Present: Practice mindfulness to stay present and fully appreciate the positive moments in your life.

Gratitude Meditation: Incorporate gratitude into your meditation practice by focusing on the things you are grateful for.

4. Acts of Kindness:

Helping Others: Engage in acts of kindness to express gratitude for the good things in your life by paying it forward.

Volunteering: Volunteer in your community to gain perspective and appreciation for the positive aspects of your own life.

Real-life examples of practicing gratitude illustrate its powerful impact on students' lives. By incorporating gratitude into daily routines, students can improve their mental health, strengthen relationships, build emotional resilience, and boost self-esteem. Practicing gratitude helps shift focus from negative thoughts to positive ones, fostering a more optimistic and fulfilling outlook on life.

#1 Piece of Advice

Here's my biggest advice to middle and high school students who are pessimistic and like giving up: Instead of focusing on the negative aspects of your life, practice gratitude for the positive things. It may sound simple, but this shift in mindset can make a world of difference in how you perceive yourself and your circumstances.

Reflection Questions:

1. How does gratitude influence your daily experience?
2. Which areas of life deserve more appreciation?
3. How might increased gratitude affect your relationships?
4. What prevents you from practicing regular gratitude?
5. How can you maintain gratitude during challenges?

Chapter Summary

▶ Practice gratitude for the positive aspects of your life.

▶ Surround yourself with positive influences.

▶ Shift your mindset by focusing on the good and expressing gratitude.

▶ Choose to surround yourself with people who lift you up and support your goals.

▶ Seek out opportunities that bring joy and fulfillment.

As we close the chapter on practicing gratitude, we must also address the mistake of focusing solely on the results. Dwelling on outcomes can sometimes hinder our ability to appreciate the journey and the lessons learned. Let's explore how embracing the process can lead to a more fulfilling and meaningful life.

FINAL THOUGHTS

Adopting these ten strategies and practicing gratitude can significantly strengthen your mindset and help you navigate the challenges of middle and high school with confidence. Remember, your journey is unique. By focusing on your growth, embracing positivity, and seeking support when needed, you can overcome self-doubt and build a bright, fulfilling future. Believe in yourself and the limitless possibilities that lie ahead.

CONCLUSION

Congratulations! You've reached the end of Rise Above: Ten Ways to Strengthen Your Mindset as a Teenager. I hope you're feeling empowered and ready to take on the world. You've just learned how to overcome self-doubt, build confidence, challenge negative thoughts, and reframe them into positive ones. The journey towards improved self-confidence and self-esteem starts from within, and you've taken the first step towards a more positive and fulfilling life.

As a teenager, facing challenges and feeling like you're not measuring up is normal. You might feel like a failure or that you'll never be good enough. But let me tell you, those negative thoughts are nothing but lies. You have the power within you to rise above those feelings and become the best version of yourself.

As you close this book, I encourage you to implement the practical advice, tips, and tricks you've learned throughout its pages. Don't just let this knowledge sit in your mind—put it into action. When you catch yourself having negative thoughts, challenge them. Reframe them into positive affirmations. Remind yourself of your strengths and all the fantastic things you've accomplished. You have so much potential, and it's time to start believing in yourself.

Now is the time to step out of your comfort zone and tackle life's problems head-on. Take risks, set goals, and work towards achieving them. Remember, failure is not the end—it's a lesson. With a strong mindset and the right attitude, you can learn and grow from your failures.

Surround yourself with positive influences—friends, family, mentors—who lift you up and encourage you to be the best version of yourself. Seek out opportunities to learn and grow, and never stop believing in your abilities. You have the power within you to achieve greatness.

To my fellow teenagers, I urge you to take what you've learned and put it into practice. Believe in yourself, challenge your negative thoughts, and rise above any obstacle that comes your way. You have the strength and resilience to overcome anything. It's time to embrace your potential and live the life you've always dreamed of.

You are not a failure. You are capable, talented, and worthy of success. Go out there and show the world just how amazing you are. I believe in you, and I can't wait to see the incredible things you'll achieve.

Now go forth and conquer. Your journey to a positive mindset and a successful life starts now. You've got this!

GLOSSARY FOR RISE ABOVE

Ten Ways to Strengthen Your Mindset as a Teenager:

1. Affirmations - Positive statements that help challenge self-sabotaging thoughts and reinforce a more positive self-image. Affirmations are vital in overcoming negative self-talk and fostering belief in one's strengths.

2. Belief in Oneself - Confidence in one's own abilities and judgment.

3. Courage - the ability to confront fear, uncertainty, and intimidation. Courage is essential when dealing with self-doubt, as it motivates individuals to step outside their comfort zones, take risks, and ultimately prove their capabilities.

4. Empathy - The capacity to understand and share the feelings of others, fostering deeper connections and relationships.

5. Empowerment - The process of gaining confidence and strength to take control of one's own life and decisions. It involves recognizing one's abilities and resources, setting boundaries, and reinforcing a sense of self-worth by actively pursuing goals and overcoming obstacles.

6. Facing Fears - Actively confronting and working through fears to reduce anxiety and boost personal growth. Facing fears is essential for breaking through limitations and gaining self-assurance.

7. Gratitude—Recognizing and appreciating the positive aspects of life. Practicing gratitude helps individuals shift focus from what is lacking to what is abundant, fostering a more optimistic mindset.

8. Growth Mindset - The belief that abilities and intelligence can be developed through hard work and dedication. A growth mindset encourages individuals to embrace challenges and view failures as opportunities for learning and growth.

9. Optimism - Having a positive outlook on life and expecting good outcomes. Optimism helps individuals see opportunities for growth and improvement even when facing self-doubt or failure. One can shift toward a more positive and empowered perspective by cultivating optimism.

10. Perseverance- The quality of continuing to pursue a course of action despite obstacles or discouragement. It is crucial in overcoming self-doubt and failure, demonstrating the determination to work toward success even in challenging circumstances.

11. Pessimism- Pessimism is a mindset or attitude characterized by a tendency to focus on the negative aspects of situations, expecting unfavorable outcomes, or believing that bad things are more likely to happen than good things. It often involves a lack of confidence in the future or in the potential for positive results. Pessimists may view challenges as insurmountable, attribute setbacks to lasting and pervasive causes, and struggle to see opportunities in difficulties.

While pessimism can sometimes serve as a protective mechanism to prepare for or avoid disappointment, chronic or excessive pessimism can hinder personal growth, decision-making, and relationships by fostering a defeatist outlook.

12. Positive Affirmations - Constructive statements reinforcing one's self-worth and abilities.

13. Positive Self-Talk—Speaking to oneself positively and encouragingly to counteract negative thinking. Positive self-talk helps shift focus away from failure and reinforces self-confidence and optimism.

14. Practicing Gratitude - The intentional practice of recognizing and appreciating the positive aspects of life.

15. Resilience - The ability to bounce back from setbacks and challenges. Resilience allows individuals to persevere through adversity and maintain forward momentum despite obstacles. It involves cultivating a positive mindset, learning from failures, and developing strategies to cope with challenges.

16. Self-Compassion - Treating oneself with kindness and understanding, especially in moments of struggle or failure. Self-compassion means offering oneself the same care one would offer a friend and being supportive in the face of imperfections. It is essential in overcoming self-doubt and building lasting confidence.

17. Self-Doubt - The feeling of uncertainty or lack of confidence in oneself and one's abilities. It is the persistent voice that questions our worth and capability. Overcoming self-doubt involves recognizing and challenging negative thoughts, building self-worth, and strengthening belief in one's potential.

18. Self-Improvement - The ongoing process of developing and enhancing one's skills, knowledge, and character. Self-improvement is key to building confidence and achieving personal growth over time.

19. Self-Validation - Recognizing and accepting one's own feelings, thoughts, and beliefs as valid.

20. Self-Worth - The internal sense of being good enough and worthy of love, success, and belonging. Self-worth is not dependent on external validation but rather a deep belief in one's inherent value.

21. Setting Goals—The process of identifying specific objectives to achieve provides direction and motivation. Setting realistic, incremental goals builds confidence and leads to measurable progress.

22. Social Support - The perception and reality of being cared for by others in one's social network. Social support can provide emotional strength, encouragement, and perspective during challenging times.

23. Support System - A network of people who provide emotional, instrumental, or informational support in times of need.

24. Visualization - Mentally creating images of success and achievement to enhance motivation and performance. Visualization can help individuals build confidence by envisioning themselves overcoming obstacles.

25. Willpower—The strength to resist short-term temptations and distractions and achieve long-term goals. Willpower is essential in maintaining focus and perseverance in the face of challenges.

26. Working Through Setbacks—This involves Using setbacks and failures as learning opportunities rather than roadblocks. It involves a constructive approach to dealing with challenges and turning them into stepping stones for growth.

Copyright Page

Rise Above: Ten Ways to Strengthen Your Mindset As A Teenager

For permission requests, write to the publisher at the address below:

CGO Publishing LLC
contact@cgopublishing.com
For more information, visit: www.cgopublishing.com

This book is a work of nonfiction. Any references to historical events, real people, or places are fictitious. Other names, characters, places, and events are products of the author's imagination. Any resemblance to actual persons, living or dead, is purely coincidental.

First Edition: 2025
ISBN: 979-8-9925817-0-6

Printed in the United States of America.

Cover design by CGO Publishing LLC.
Interior design by CGO Publishing LLC.

www.ingramcontent.com/pod-product-compliance
Lightning Source LLC
Chambersburg PA
CBHW061658120626

46550CB00003B/988